THE HOLY MOUNTAIN

BY THE SAME AUTHOR

BYZANTINE SACRED ART

ANCHORED IN GOD

MODERN GREEK PHILOSOPHERS
ON THE HUMAN SOUL

BYZANTINE THOUGHT AND ART

MODERN GREEK THOUGHT

ST. COSMAS AITOLOS

ST. MACARIOS OF CORINTH

ST. NICODEMOS THE HAGIORITE

ST. GREGORY PALAMAS
Fresco, Monastery of Dionysiou.
XVIth century.

THE HOLY MOUNTAIN

Two lectures on Mount Athos, of which the first
deals with its Scholars, Missionaries and Saints,
and the second with its Music, Musicians, and
Hymnographers; together with an account of a
Recent Visit to Athos

BY

CONSTANTINE CAVARNOS

INSTITUTE FOR BYZANTINE
AND MODERN GREEK STUDIES
115 Gilbert Road
Belmont, Massachusetts 02178
U. S. A.

Copyright, © 1973, by Constantine Cavarnos
Published by THE INSTITUTE FOR BYZANTINE
AND MODERN GREEK STUDIES, INC.
115 Gilbert Road, Belmont, Massachusetts 02178
Library of Congress Catalog Card Number: 73-84103
ISBN   0-914744-38-0

Second edition 1977

Third printing 1988

PREFACE

The three parts into which this book is divided were originally written on three different occasions. Part One, entitled *Scholars, Missionaries, and Saints,* is a lecture that was sponsored by the Yale Orthodox Christian Movement and was delivered at Yale University on October 21, 1968. Part Two — *Music, Musicians, and Hymnographers* — was written at the invitation of the Colgate International Students Forum and of the Colgate Orthodox Christian Fellowship for a symposium on Mount Athos that was organized by them, and was read at Colgate University on May 15, 1969. Both have been considerably augmented throughout for inclusion in this volume. Part Three — *Recent Visit to Athos* — was written during my 1965 sojourn on Athos and has subsequently been amplified at certain points by the addition of significant new material that has come to my attention.

To these I have added a *Menologium of Athonite Saints* — a list of the saints of the Holy Mountain according to the months when their memory is celebrated. Further, I have added a *Glossary* explaining numerous terms used in the book, and a *Bibliography* which lists the works that I have found especially helpful in the preparation of this volume.

Part One is the first comprehensive account of the scholars, missionaries and saints of Mount Athos; while Part Two is similarly the first attempt to discuss Athonite music, musicians and hymnographers in a somewhat extensive and systematic manner. The account of my 1965 pilgrimage, while having analogues in other books about Athos, brings to light new data and perspectives, and communicates important messages from the holy fathers who dwell there regarding "Ecumenism," Orthodox monasticism in the contemporary world, and other topics. The Menologium, the first that has been composed, provides a helpful reference list for the general reader, and should be of use to the Orthodox clergy for celebrating these saints, a great many of whom are not mentioned in the liturgical books named *Menaia*.

A word should be said about the spelling of Greek names and words. As regards the names of persons, I have in general followed the phonetics of the modern Greek language. In the case of the titles of books, in transliterating them in the Notes, in the Bibliography, and occasionally in the text, I have followed the method which is employed by English scholars and which I explain at the beginning of the Glossary of my book *Byzantine Thought and Art* (1968).

I am very grateful to Dr. John Johnstone, Jr., and to Professor Leo M. Pruden of Brown University for reading the entire manuscript and making many helpful comments.

CONSTANTINE CAVARNOS

May, 1973

CONTENTS

PREFACE vii

LIST OF ILLUSTRATIONS xi

P A R T   O N E

SCHOLARS, MISSIONARIES, AND SAINTS

INTRODUCTORY 15

I   SCHOLARS 17

II   MISSIONARIES 43

III   SAINTS 60

EPILOGUE 73

P A R T   T W O

MUSIC, MUSICIANS, AND HYMNOGRAPHERS

I   MUSIC 77

II   MUSICIANS AND HYMNOGRAPHERS 85

PART THREE

RECENT VISIT TO ATHOS

I	ON THE WAY	93
II	MONASTERY OF XEROPOTAMOU	96
III	A RUMANIAN HERMIT	99
IV	ST. NICODEMOS' LAST ABODE	101
V	RUSSIAN SKETE OF ST. ANDREW	104
VI	MONASTERY OF KOUTLOUMOUSIOU	108
VII	MONASTERY OF GRIGORIOU	110
VIII	MONASTERY OF DIONYSIOU	115
IX	SKETE OF ST. ANNE	121
X	THE NEW SKETE	123
XI	MONASTERY OF ST. PAUL	126
XII	CONCLUDING POSTSCRIPT	128
	NOTES	133
	APPENDIX A: MENOLOGIUM OF ATHONITE SAINTS	146
	APPENDIX B: GLOSSARY	154
	SELECTED BIBLIOGRAPHY	160
	INDEX	163

ILLUSTRATIONS

Plate

Saint Gregory Palamas, Monastery of Dionysiou. Fresco.

Frontispiece

1. Saint Athanasios the Athonite, Church of the Protaton at Karyes, Mount Athos. Fresco by Panselinos.

2. Saint Antony Pechersky. Drawing based on an early Russian panel icon.

3. Saint Nil Sorsky. Russian icon.

4. A composition of John Koukouzelis in old Byzantine notation.

5. Saint John Koukouzelis. Copy of an icon in a manuscript of the Monastery of Lavra.

6. Saint Symeon Nemanya, Church of Studenitza, Yugoslavia. Fresco.

7. Saint Sava, Archbishop of Serbia, Church of Milesevo, Yugoslavia. Fresco.

8. Saint Nikephoros the Solitary. Icon drawn by Fotis Kontoglou.

9. Saint Niphon, Patriarch of Constantinople. Fresco.

10. Saint Dionysios the Orator. Icon drawn by Kontoglou.

11. Saint Maximos the Greek. Panel icon.

12. Saint Cosmas Aitolos. Panel icon.

13. Saint Nicodemos The Hagiorite. Icon drawn by Kontoglou.

14. Monastery of St. Paul.

15. Map of the Peninsula of the Holy Mountain.

16. Joseph the Hesychast. Photograph.

PART ONE

SCHOLARS, MISSIONARIES, AND SAINTS

INTRODUCTORY

Mount Athos, also known as the Holy Mountain, is the largest and by far the most important community of Eastern Orthodox monks in the world. It consists of twenty monasteries, a dozen sketes, numerous small hermitages scattered over a thirty-five mile long peninsula, and a centrally located capital, Karyes. This peninsula is in northern Greece, about five hours by bus southeast of Thessaloniki (Salonica). It is known as the Mountain, because its terrain is hilly and rises near its southern extremity to nearly 6,500 feet above the sea level.

All the monks who dwell on the Holy Mountain are, according to the 1926 Constitutional Charter, Greek subjects. But they are of different nationalities. The great majority are natives of Greece; the rest are Russians, Serbs, Bulgarians, and Rumanians. The relative percentages of the monks of these nationalities can be judged by the fact that seventeen of the monasteries are Greek, one is Bulgarian, one Russian and one Serbian, while seven of the sketes are Greek, two are Russian, two Rumanian, and one Bulgarian. A skete is typically a settlement of hermits in the neighborhood of a common church, known as the *kyriakon,* because the hermits assemble here for common worship on *Kyriake,* Sunday. All the monasteries trace their establishment to Byzantine times. The oldest is Lavra, founded in 963. A few of the others, such as Vatopedi and Iviron, were founded soon after.

Many books have been written about the Holy Mountain by Greeks, Russians, Englishmen, Germans, French and others. These books deal mainly with the history of the monasteries, their architecture, iconography, manuscripts, and contemporary conditions of living. I myself have written a book, *Anchored in God,* dealing with these aspects of Athos. No comprehensive book or article,

however, has been written on the subject of the scholars, missionaries and saints of the Holy Mountain. There are references to some
of them in most books on Athos, but these references are usually
rather brief or even quite incidental. Occasionally one will find a
chapter or section devoted to some scholar, missionary or saint, or
to several, but the rest, often the more significant, are not even mentioned.

My investigations on this subject over a period of years have
shown that while the known Athonite missionaries have been few,
the role they have played in Orthodox Christendom has been extremely important; and that the scholars and saints have been
numerous, some of them very influential. I shall discuss those who
have been of special significance for the Orthodox world in general
and for Orthodox monasticism in particular. My aim in doing this
is to call attention to the tremendously important role that Mount
Athos has played among the Orthodox as a great workshop in
holiness and a center of spiritual enlightenment radiating far and
wide.

CHAPTER I

SCHOLARS

I begin with a discussion of the scholars of Athos. By scholars (*logioi*) here I mean learned monks who have written extensively on matters pertaining to the Orthodox faith. I do not mean individuals who preoccupied themselves with inquiry motivated merely by intellectual curiosity or by the desire to make "informative" or "original" contributions to the academic world. The latter conception of a scholar is alien to Orthodox monasticism. The aim of Athonite scholars in writing has always been to edify their fellow Christians. Their scholarship has been motivated by authentic Christian love. Insofar as their learning was used for edification, these scholars may be said to have been missionaries. However, I have reserved the term missionaries for those monks who traveled beyond Mount Athos and occupied themselves with the enlightenment, spiritual awakening and regeneration of their brethren in other regions by preaching, teaching, counseling, confessing, and in some instances by writing and publishing as well.

Most of the famous scholars of Athos flourished in the 14th and 18th centuries. To the 14th century belong the following, who were both scholars and great practicing mystics: St. Nikephoros the Solitary, Theoleptos of Philadelphia, St. Gregory Palamas, St. Philotheos the Patriarch, St. Callistos Xanthopoulos, and Ignatios Xanthopoulos; to the 18th century, Dionysios of Fourna, Neophytos Kafsokalyvitis, Theocletos Karatzas, Kaisarios Dapontes, and St. Nicodemos the Hagiorite. The most important scholars of the intervening period were Maximos the Greek (16th century) and Agapios Landos, also known as Agapios the Cretan (17th century). After the 18th century, the most noteworthy scholars of the Holy Mountain are Bartholomew of Koutloumousiou and Constantine Doukakis in the 19th century, and in our time Gabriel and Theocletos of

Dionysiou and Vasilii Krivosheine of Panteleimonos. I shall discuss these scholars in chronological order.

1. St. Nikephoros the Solitary

A native of Southern Italy, Nikephoros the Solitary left his native land, embraced Orthodoxy, and went into monastic seclusion on Mount Athos. Having received spiritual instruction here and learned also from personal experience the ways of Orthodox mysticism, he became a spiritual guide of others, through both the spoken and the written word. Among his disciples were Theoleptos and Gregory Palamas, Archbishop of Thessaloniki. The latter speaks highly of Nikephoros in his work *In Defense of Those who Practice Inner Silence*.[1] Nikephoros wrote a discourse entitled *Concerning Inner Wakefulness and Guarding of the Heart*,[2] which is included in the *Philokalia*, a monumental book of the Eastern Church containing selections from the writings of some thirty masters of the spiritual life.[3] He also wrote a treatise on the Orthodox faith which remains unpublished.

Speaking briefly about his life and discourse *Concerning Inner Wakefulness*, his biographer in the Greek *Philokalia*, Nicodemos the Hagiorite, says: "Our most holy Father Nikephoros, who led a life of spiritual endeavor on the Holy Mountain of Athos, and was in his prime a little before 1340, became a teacher and mystagogue of Gregory of Thessaloniki in the sublime lessons of ascetic philosophy, as the latter somewhere testifies. Through a life of silence free from cares, devoted to the inner law, he attained ineffable union with the ultramundane and supreme Being, and experienced in his heart the true illumination of Grace. Having become richly filled with this deifying gift, the Blessed man imparted it to us paternally and abundantly, through the present tract, so that if we wish we might be equally rewarded. He gathered here together the passages in the lives of the Holy Fathers that speak of inner wakefulness, attention and prayer, and added from his own experience the natural and truly scientific method of drawing the mind within the heart through breathing and of invoking the Lord Jesus during the inhalation. Thus he provided for the first time a most precise rule for the practice of holy inner wakefulness and a ladder of pure, undistracted prayer and of the gifts that spring from it."

Nikephoros was exiled for a time from the Holy Mountain by the emperor Michael Palaiologos, because he opposed the union of the Eastern Church with the Western that was decided by the Second Council of Lyon (1274).

His memory is celebrated on May 4. The following couplet is recited then, calling attention to his chief contribution:

"We thank thee, O Father Nikephoros,
For the art of prayer, which thou didst hand down to us."

2. *Theoleptos of Philadelphia*

Theoleptos (*c.* 1250-1324/26), a native of Nicaea, led the life of an anchorite on Mount Athos and afterwards (*c.* 1284) was ordained Metropolitan of Philadelphia, Asia Minor. He was deeply influenced by the mystical teaching of Nikephoros the Solitary. Like him, he wrote instructions on the inward life, and personally instructed Gregory Palamas in the practice of inner attention and mental prayer. A tract of his, entitled *Discourse Explaining the Inner Work according to Christ and Indicating briefly the Discipline of the Monastic Vocation*,[4] appears in the *Philokalia*. He wrote many other works, including letters and hymns, but most of them remain unpublished.

In the biographical note on Theoleptos that is contained in the *Philakalia,* we read: "Theoleptos, the really Great luminary of Philadelphia, was in his prime during the reign of Andronikos II Palaiologos, about 1325. Having first led and anchoritic life on the Holy Mountain, and subsequently taken up the spiritual leadership of Philadelphia, he became the guide and mystagogue of Saint Gregory of Thessaloniki in the most beautiful of subjects. He instructed him in the practice of holy inner wakefulness and mental prayer when Gregory was still a layman, as we read in the life of this same Gregory written by Philotheos the Patriarch. These discourses, which have been written by him, are an excellent sketch and a strict rule of the hidden meditation in Christ, composed with divine thoughts and clarity of expression in a masterly manner. They are most useful and important for those who want to receive concise instruction in the divine science of spiritual philosophy."

Being strongly opposed to the union of the Orthodox Church with the Latin, like Nikephoros, he was imprisoned for a time at Constantinople.

3. St. Gregory Palamas

The most eminent disciple of these two mystics and scholars was Gregory Palamas (1296-1359), also known as Gregory of Thessaloniki. A native of Constantinople, he renounced the world at an early age, went to Athos, and there led an arduous life of spiritual endeavor. He dwelt at the monasteries of Vatopedi, Esphigmenou, and Lavra, where he stayed the longest. Subsequently he was ordained Archbishop of Thessaloniki.

St. Gregory is one of the greatest mystics and theologians of the Orthodox Church, and the most renowned teacher and defender of *Hesychasm* or Orthodox mysticism in the 14th century. He wrote numerous works: antirrhetical, ascetic-mystical, dogmatic, pastoral, hymnographic, etc. A few of his ascetic-mystical writings are contained in the *Philokalia*. In his biographical sketch contained in this work we read:

"Our Father Saint Gregory of Thessaloniki was in his prime during the reign of Andronikos II Palaiologos, about 1340. Renouncing the world and all worldly things, he left his native place, Constantinople, and went to the Holy Mountain of Athos, where he embraced the monastic life. Here, practicing very strict forms of discipline, and alone contemplating God alone, through extreme inner quiet he became a most Godlike mirror of the Holy Spirit, having risen to the supreme height of practice and contemplation. His intellect having been illuminated by divine effulgences, he left to the Church of God writings of surpassing wisdom and theology, and became a pillar of Orthodoxy. The excerpts contained in the present book are from these works. They lure the readers to real treasures of divine knowledge, spiritual wisdom, and perfection. For this heavenly mind that beheld God not only gathered together what had been said by older Saints, but added what he had come to know through long experience and blessed feeling. He developed out of these an offering of manifest beauty pertaining to the interior life; and thus no one will ever consider these as products of the human intellect. . . . By means of them he vigorously defends those who occupy themselves with holy quiet, inner attention and mental prayer, and argues very cogently against the empty talking of those opposed, bringing forth proofs from Scripture."

Palamas took up the defense of Orthodox mysticism against the Westernizing monks, Barlaam and Akindynos, who attacked and ridiculed it. In this dispute he emerged victorious. His teaching was declared sound by four Synods which met at Constantinople: two in 1341, another in 1351, and a fourth in 1368, while that of Barlaam and Akindynos was condemned. The Synod of 1368 proclaimed Gregory, who had died nine years earlier, a saint.

The very high esteem in which he has been held since then by the Orthodox is vividly expressed by the following apolytikion, which is chanted in his honor on the Second Sunday of Great Lent, when the Church commemorates him:

"Thou luminary of Orthodoxy, pillar and teacher
of the Church, the glory of the monastics, the
invincible champion of theologians, O Gregory
miracle-worker, the boast of Thessaloniki, the
preacher of Grace, entreat God perpetually for
the salvation of our souls."

His great importance for Orthodoxy has received increasing recognition in recent times. This is testified by the fact that the first critical edition of his collected works began to be published in Greece in 1962, under the sponsorship of the Royal Institute of Research, and by the appearance of a good number of articles and books by Orthodox theologians dealing with his teaching.[5]

4. St. Philotheos the Patriarch

Born in Thessaloniki, Philotheos (*c*. 1300-*c*. 1379) was tonsured a monk at an early age. After living for a time on Mount

Sinai, he went to Athos, where he became abbot of the Monastery of Lavra. In 1347 he was ordained Metropolitan of Heracleia in Thrace, and in 1353 he became Patriarch of Constantinople. He served as Patriarch until 1354, and again from 1364 to 1376. Both while on Athos and subsequently, Philotheos wrote religious works that evidence wide learning as well as profound understanding and spirituality. Many of his writings are antirrhetical in nature, directed against scoffers of hesychasm such as Akindynos, Barlaam, and Gregoras. Twelve of his discourses against Gregoras appear in Migne's *Patrologia Graeca*.[6] The rest of his antirrhetical discourses remain unpublished.[7] In connection with hesychasm, noteworthy also is the fact that it was Philotheos who ordained that its foremost defender, Gregory Palamas, be commemorated on the Second Sunday of Great Lent, and that he composed an akoluthia for this occasion.

Other important works by Philotheos are a series of lives of saints, particularly of those saints of the Holy Mountain who were his contemporaries — e.g. Gregory Palamas, Germanos of Lavra, Isidore the Patriarch, Savvas of Vatopedi; and encomia to his spiritual father St. Nicodemos the Younger, St. Demetrios, the Holy Apostles, the Three Hierarchs (Basil the Great, Gregory of Nazianzus, and John Chrysostom), and to All the Saints. Several of the latter remain unpublished. He also wrote hymns, hermeneutic and liturgical works, not all of which have appeared in print.

5. *St. Callistos Xanthopoulos and Ignatios Xanthopoulos*

The two other very noteworthy scholars of the 14th century, Callistos Xanthopoulos (d. 1363) and Ignatios Xanthopoulos (fl. 1360) were, like Palamas, natives of Constantinople. They, too, renounced the world at an early age.

More is known about Callistos than Ignatios. Callistos is said to have been a pupil of St. Gregory the Sinaite, who was a great mystic and theologian. This Gregory lived on Mount Athos for a time and instructed many in the practice of spiritual prayer. In 1397, after twenty-eight years here, at the Monastery of the Xanthopouloi, which appears to be identical with the Monastery of Pantocratoros, Callistos was made Patriarch of Constantinople. *

In collaboration with Ignatios, who was a close friend of his, he wrote a treatise entitled *Strict Method and Rule for Those Who Choose to Live in Silence Monastically*,[8] which gives detailed instructions for those who aspire to attain spiritual perfection. This work is included in the *Philokalia* and is accompanied by a discourse *On Prayer*[9] written by Callistos.

Symeon of Thessaloniki says this about Callistos and Ignatios and their book in his discussion of the Jesus Prayer: "In our own time, moved by the Spirit, these two men, our Father Saint Callistos, who became Patriarch of New Rome, and his intimate fellow spiritual striver, the holy Ignatios, who were truly God-inspired, God-bearing, Christ-bearing and divine, wrote about this prayer. They authored a book, a product of spiritual, very sublime, divine wisdom, setting forth in one hundred chapters a perfect knowledge of it."[10]

On November 22nd the Orthodox Church commemorates "our holy father Callistos," believed by Nicodemos the Hagiorite and other compilers of Lives Saints to be Callistos Xanthopoulos; and the following couplet is recited in honor of him:

"Callistos, having overthrown the most wicked enemy,
Approaches God as a select friend."

6. *Maximos the Greek*

Maximos of Vatopedi, better known as Maximos the Greek (*c.* 1470-1556), is the next very remarkable Athonite scholar. He was born in Arta, in western Greece. After completing his general education in his native city, he went to Italy for higher studies. He spent about fifteen years studying at various Italian universities the ancient Greek and Latin language and literature, Platonic and Aristotelian philosophy, and privately numerous Christian writings. Upon leaving Italy, he went to the Monastery of Vatopedi on Mount Athos. He was thirty-six years old at that time.

At Vatopedi, he stayed for ten years. During this period he greatly enriched his knowledge and understanding of Orthodoxy by studying the manuscripts in Vatopedi's excellent library and through strict monastic discipline. Also, he took part in missions to various parts of Greece and other Balkan countries. The aim of these mis-

sions was to solicit financial help; but Maximos used them as opportunities for vigorous preaching, seeking to effect the regeneration
of the Orthodox and to counteract Roman Catholic propaganda.

In 1518, at the insistent invitation of the Russian monarch Basil
Ivanovich, he went to Moscow to correct the liturgical and other
books of the Russian Church. He spent in Russia the remaining
thirty-eight years of his life.

Maximos' contributions to the Church of Russia and to Russian
spirituality were of the greatest importance. Thus, he made a translation of the *Psalter* from Greek into Russian that was approved by
the Metropolitan Barlaam and was disseminated throughout Russia.
He corrected the other liturgical books of the Russian Church, translated many writings of the Greek Fathers into Slavonic, and wrote a
large number of books in the fields of apologetics, dogmatics, exegesis, Christian ethics and other fields of religion. As an apologist of
Orthodoxy, he defended the Russian Church against the claims of
Rome, criticized the rationalistic teachings of the Western Reformation as well as Judaism and Islam. In addition, he sought to reform
Russian monasticism and religious life in general, as these had
become infected with secularism. He thus succeeded in ushering
into Russia a spiritual awakening and enlightenment of great pro-
portions.

The work of Maximos aroused strong antagonisms in certain
quarters. He was branded a heretic and treated very badly. But with
the passage of time he and his work gained wider and wider recognition. And a century after his death the Church of Russia declared
him a saint. The following hymn is chanted in his honor by the
Russian Orthodox on January 21st, when they commemorate him:

> "Having been made resplendent by the glory of
> the Spirit, thou hast been deemed worthy of
> the wisdom of those who speak with eloquence
> and knowledge of things divine. Having il-
> luminated with the light of piety the hearts of
> men that were in the darkness of ignorance, thou
> didst appear as a great luminary of Orthodoxy,
> O Saint Maximos. And having left thy father-

land out of divine zeal, thou didst become a settler in the Russian lands, where the right hand of
the Most High crowned thee in the midst of the
suffering of fetters and of prison and glorified
thee in miracles. Intercede unceasingly for us,
who with love honor thy memory."

A bulky volume, entitled *Maximos the Greek*,[11] written by
Gregory Papamichael (1874-1956), distinguished professor of theology at the University of Athens, appeared in 1950. It gives a full
account of Maximos' life, character, and work.

7. *Agapios Landos*

The most notable scholar of the Holy Mountain in the 17th
century is Agapios Landos, also known as Agapios the Cretan.
Landos was born in Crete towards the end of the 16th century or
the beginning of the 17th, and died in Venice between 1664 and
1671. He received his education first in his native island and then
on Mount Athos, where he was helped by learned monks and had
access to many fine libraries. Among the subjects in which he acquired proficiency were Italian, Latin, and apparently also Arabic.

At Athos he chose the hermit's life, settling in a hut at the
community of hermitages named Small Skete of Saint Anne, a
dependency of the Monastery of Lavra. Here he devoted his time
assiduously to prayer, study, and writing. Leading such a life, he
became, as the historian Zaviras remarks, "a wise, industrious, virtuous and saintly man."[12]

Agapios' stay on Athos was interrupted by journeys to Venice,
where he went to print his books (as printers were forbidden in
Greece), and to various parts of Greece as a missionary to his
fellow Christians. His activities as an itinerant preacher were very
fruitful. Springing from deep religious faith, spiritual wisdom and
a holy life, and conveyed in a language that could be understood
by all, his teaching and exhortations had a profound effect on his
audiences.

More than a dozen books were authored, compiled or translated by Landos. Except for one, which is on agriculture, all of

them are religious. His most popular work to this day is *The Salvation of Sinners*.[13] From 1641, when it first appeared in print, to the middle of the 19th century, it went into over ten editions. And since then it has been reprinted again and again. Augustine Kantiotis, Metropolitan of Phlorina in northwestern Greece, remarks about this book: "*The Salvation of Sinners*, a work of the hieromonk Agapios the Cretan, written in simple and living language, with very vivid examples and illustrations, was the most cherished reading of the Greek people during the period of Turkish Rule. As a result of reading this book, many souls were saved. . . . And to this day it has not ceased touching profoundly simple souls, which in the pages of this book find a pure fount of Orthodox teaching, based on Holy Scripture and Sacred Tradition."[14] Its popularity has not been restricted to the Greeks. It enjoyed considerable popularity among the Russians also, having been translated into Russian probably by Paissy Velichkovsky (1722-1794) or his followers,[15] and has also appeared in Arabic and Rumanian translations.[16]

Among Agapios' other books, those that have been especially popular are the *Soul-Saving Psalter*,[17] *New Paradise*,[18] *Eklogion*,[19] and *Kalokairine*.[20] The first is a translation of the Psalter based on the interpretation of the Psalms made in the 5th century by Theodoret of Cyrus. It went into over ten editions from 1643, when it was first published, to 1821; and it still circulates. *New Paradise* contains the lives of many men and women saints taken from the works of the Byzantine hagiographer Symeon Metaphrastes (10th century), translated by Landos into the Greek vernacular. This work has been translated into Rumanian.[21] *Eklogion* contains the most beautiful lives of saints selected from the works of the same hagiographer and translated by Landos into the modern Greek idiom; while *Kalokairine* comprises the most beautiful lives of saints celebrated in the summer season (*kalokairi*), from March 1st to August 31st, similarly translated.

The Cretan monk believed very strongly in the value of reading the lives of saints. In the Preface of *New Paradise*, he observes: "A person is touched more profoundly and benefits more by reading one beautiful life of a Saint than by discourses and philosophies."

Landos' other works include *Guidance of Christians*,[22] *Sunday*

Sermonary,[23] consisting of sermons for every Sunday of the year selected from various writers of the Church, and *Theotokarion,*[24] containing beautiful and joyful hymns to the Theotokos selected from books of the Holy Mountain.

All of Agapios' religious works have been popular and have been reprinted many times. Being very edifying, and written in a charming style and — with the exception of the hymnographical books — in the common language, they were for two centuries the chief reading of the Greek people.[25]

8. *Dionysios of Fourna*

The 18th century was a high point in Athonite scholarship, as well as in moral and spiritual vigor, rivaling the 14th. Archimandrite Gabriel, abbot of the Monastery of Dionysiou, excellently notes this fact in the following passage of his book *Lausaikon of the Holy Mountain:*

"From the middle of the eighteenth century there began a spiritual endeavor which soon created the movement for bringing back the institution of Coenobitism in the holy monasteries, arousing the aspiration for learning, awakening the Greek people and transmitting to them the truths of Christianity through the publication of the writings of the Fathers in simple idiom and through sermons. This movement produced fruits which in both quality and quantity surpassed those of all other periods of Hagiorite life."[26]

The first notable scholar of this period is the hieromonk Dionysios of Fourna (1670-*c.* 1745). Dionysios went to Athos at the age of sixteen and became a monk at the Skete of Karyes. Here he greatly broadened the knowledge he had received at Fourna, Thessaly, and mastered the art of painting icons according to the Byzantine tradition. His frescoes and panel icons show him to have been one of the more remarkable iconographers of that time.

Besides painting icons, Dionysios occupied himself with writing. He composed epigrams, two akoluthias, and a book entitled *Explanation of the Art of Painting,*[27] referred to by English writers as the *Painter's Guide,* or *Byzantine Guide to Painting.* He is best

known as the author of this book, which he wrote about 1730.
Drawing from Byzantine manuscripts as well as directly from the
many treasures of Byzantine iconography on the Holy Mountain,
Dionysios here explains the technique of painting icons in the
Byzantine style on walls and panels, and gives instructions as to how
each saint or scene should be depicted.

His famous book was translated in the last century into French
by Paul Durand, and was published with an Introduction and
numerous notes by Adolphe N. Didron under the title *Manuel
d'iconographie chretienne.*[28] And an English translation of the
Second Part is contained in Margaret Stokes' *Christian Iconography.*[29]

Dionysios was, in his way, a missionary, too. He established a
nunnery in Fourna, a monastery near this town, a school and a
workshop of iconography close to the monastery.

9. *Neophytos Kafsokalyvitis*

The next important 18th century scholar is Neophytos Kafsoka-
livitis, also known as Neophytos the Peloponnesian and Neophytos
of Jewish Origin (*c.* 1702-1780). He was born of Jewish parents at
Patras, in the Peloponnesos, and was educated at Constantinople,
Patmos and Iannina. According to his own statement, made in the
Preface of his book *Confutation of the Religion of the Jews,*[30] Neophytos was a teacher of the Jews, a Rabbi, when he was converted
to Orthodox Christianity at the age of thirty-eight.

After his conversion he went to Mount Athos and was tonsured
a monk. He dwelt at Kafsokalyvia, a settlement of hermits that is
under the jurisdiction of the Monastery of Lavra. This led to his
becoming known as Kafsokalyvitis.

In 1749, he established together with others the Athonias
Academy — a school of higher learning — under the auspices of
the Monastery of Vatopedi, and became its first director.

Having dwelt on the Holy Mountain for many years, he left
and taught first in Chios and then at the Greek school of Bucharest,
where he spent the rest of his life. A religious, moral and intellectual
renaissance was taking place among the Greeks, and there was a
great demand for good teachers.

Neophytos Kafsokalyvitis was not only a remarkable teacher, but also a versatile and prolific writer. Most of the works he authored are religious. Among these are *Pilgrim's Guide to the Holy Mountain,*[31] *Against the Calvinists,*[32] *Handbook Proving that Christians Ought to Partake of the Divine Eucharist More Often,*[33] *Nomocanon or Interpretation of the Holy Canons of the Synods,*[34] and the *Confutation* mentioned above. His books on Holy Communion and on the holy canons have been his most influential. The former played a major role in the 18th century religious movement of the "Kollyvades"[35] that originated on Athos, while the latter has been an important guide in the study of Orthodox canon law. One of the most outstanding Greek theologians and churchmen of the last century, Constantine Oikonomos, speaks of the *Nomocanon* as "a very famous book, great in bulk and full of teachings pertaining to ecclesiastical questions, leading (on the whole) to the appropriate answers, adding many noteworthy explanations, organizing the subject-matter methodically and formulating it clearly and eloquently."[36] Oikonomos noted that the original manuscript of this work was at the Russian Monastery on Athos, Panteleimonos.

Neophytos' secular works include a *Commentary on Thucydides,*[37] a *Commentary on the Ethics of Aristotle,*[38] *The Philosopher or Theist,*[39] and a monumental 1400 quarto-page *Commentary on Gazis' Grammar,*[40] published in 1768 at Bucharest. This commentary was for decades employed extensively in the Greek schools, and has been praised highly by European philologists.

10. *Theocletos Karatzas*

Another scholar of this period who dwelt at Kafsokalyvia was Theocletos Karatzas (1728-1777). A native of Constantinople and a descendant of the prominent Karatzas family, he received an excellent education that prepared him for an active life. He became a man of wide learning and proficient not only in the Greek language, but also in Latin, Italian, Arabic, Syriac, Persian, and Turkish.

After completing his studies, he served first as secretary of the rulers of Wallachia, and then as secretary of the Patriarchate at Constantinople.

But yearning for an inward life of spiritual endeavor, "he renounced honors and glory," as Zaviras remarks, "and embraced the monastic life."[41] becoming a hermit at the Skete of Kafsokalyvia. Here he wrote two very valuable books in simple, demotic Greek. One of these, intended primarily for monks, is a translation of St. Basil's *Ascetic Rules*. The other, designed for confessors or spiritual guides, is a nomocanon, containing a translation of all the canons of the Orthodox Church: the Apostolic canons, those of the Synods, and those of particular Church Fathers.[42]

Theocletos died prematurely, at the age of fifty.

11. *Kaisarios Dapontes*

Kaisarios Dapontes (1714-1784) was born in the Aegean island of Skopelos, and at Holy Baptism was named Constantine. He received his primary education here over a period of six years. His teacher was a monk named Hierotheos, who had been brought to Skopelos by his father from the Athonite monastery of Iviron to open a school.

At the age of sixteen or seventeen he was sent by his father to Constantinople to continue his education and find a job. From Constantinople Dapontes went to Bucharest, where he entered the high school of that city on a scholarship. Afterward he became assistant secretary of Constantine Mavrokordatos, ruler of Wallachia, at his court in Bucharest. In 1842 he went to Constantinople, and here obtained employment as chief secretary of another prominent Phanariote, John Mavrogordatos. He remained in the service of the latter until 1747.

In 1747 false accusations were made against him to the Vizier at Constantinople, as a result of which he was sent into prison and heavily fined by the Turks. Having been released after twenty months' imprisonment, he went to the island of Halki to lead a quiet life. Here he married, but became a widower in 1751. Two years later he resolved to renounce the world and become a monk. To this end he went to a little island near Skopelos named Piperi, where a monk from Athos had established a skete. Here he was tonsured a monk and was renamed Kaisarios. Regarding this withdrawal from the world, Dapontes says the following in his largely autobiographical book *Garden of the Graces:*

"In 1753, having come to myself, I stopped and reflected on the multitude of my troubles, those at Bogdania and at Wallachia, and finally those at Constantinople — many indeed, the whole Danube could not wash me clear of them. And having seen and realized the vanity of the world, and having had my fill of the things of the world, both good and bad, and having come justly to hate the world and worldly things, I developed a love for the wilderness and fled from the world. I left Constantinople and came to Piperi, a desolate island with two churches, one old and the other new, both dedicated to the Theotokos."[43]

After a stay of three years in Piperi, he went to Athos and entered the Monastery of Xeropotamou. He remained at this monastery until 1784, when he died at the age of seventy-one. His stay at Xeropotamou was interrupted only by an eight-year begging mission to Moldavia, Bogdania, and various parts of Greece to gather money for the renovation of the monastery.

Dapontes was one of the most erudite and prolific writers of his time. He wrote at least twenty-four books, mostly in verse and composed while he was on the Holy Mountain. Among his religious books are the following: *Discourse of our Holy Father Cyril of Alexandria on the Departure of the Soul and the Second Coming of Christ, translated into the Simple Dialect;*[44] *Pearls of the Three Hierarchs, or Admonitory Discourses, translated into Simple Language;* [45] *Rational Manual, Consisting of Hymns to the Theotokos and Prayers in Various Metres and Melodies;*[46] and *Explanation of the Divine Liturgy.*[47]

Of his secular works, the best known are the *Historical Catalogue*[48] and the *Dacian Ephemerides.*[49] The latter is a chronicle of the contemporary Balkan wars. The Greek text with an annotated French translation has been published by Emile Legrand in three volumes, entitled: *Ephemerides Daces, ou Chronicles de la Guerre de Quatre Ans,* 1736-1739.[50]

Some of Dapontes' books are partly religious and partly secular, for instance, *Garden of the Graces,* which I have already mentioned, and *Mirror of Women,*[51] which contains stories about good and evil women found in the Old Testament and in secular works.

Regarding Dapontes as an author of secular writings, the following comment by a recent historian of modern Greek literature is fairly apt: "Although verbose and pedestrian, Dapontes has some talents. He is observant, he loves truth and justice; he is sincere, not at all a hypocrite."[52]

12. St. Nicodemos the Hagiorite

The greatest, most influential scholar of the Holy Mountain in the 18th century was undoubtedly Nicodemos the Hagiorite (1749-1809), who in 1955 was officially declared a saint by the Ecumenical Patriarchate at Constantinople and has become increasingly acknowledged as the foremost Orthodox theologian of the post-Byzantine period. Nicodemos was a native of Naxos, one of the Cyclades Islands. He received his elementary education at the school in Naxos. His teacher here was Archimandrite Chrysanthos Aitolos, brother of St. Cosmas Aitolos, about whom I shall speak later. When he graduated from this school he went to Smyrna, to continue his studies at the flourishing Evangeliki School. Having completed his studies at Smyrna, he returned to his native island. There he worked during the next five years as secretary of the local bishop.

At the age of twenty-six, Nicodemos went to the Monastery of Dionysiou on the Holy Mountain. He became a monk at this monastery, but did not stay here permanently. Seeking conditions most suitable for spiritual prayer and writing, he changed his residence several times. He preferred small hermitages and found the best one at the region known as Kapsala.

The literary activities of Nicodemos began in 1777, only two years after his arrival at Mount Athos, and continued for thirty-two years, until the time of his death. His writings show him to have been not only the most prolific Athonite author of the 18th century, but also the most versatile in the sphere of religion. He wrote, translated, or edited over twenty-seven books, many of them monumental, evidencing quite extraordinary erudition and remarkable insight into every phase of the Orthodox Faith. His books deal with spiritual practices, morality, confession, the holy mysteries ("sacraments"), canon law, the lives of saints, hymnography, and so on. In addition to books, he composed many akoluthias in honor of various saints and revised many that had been written by earlier Orthodox hymnographers. His poetic compositions are characterized by deep religious feeling and considerable literary merit.

Like Agapios the Cretan and Kaisarios Dapontes, in his non-liturgical works he used the vernacular, so that what he said could be understood by all. Unlike Neophytos Kafsokalyvitis and Dapontes, he wrote no secular works.

Among Nicodemos' most popular books, which have been reprinted again and again, are the *Philokalia, Confessor's Guide,*[53] *Unseen Warfare,*[54] *New Martyrologium,* [55] *Spiritual Exercises,*[56] *Rudder,*[57] and *Handbook of Counsel.*[58] The *Philokalia,* which was first published in 1782 at Venice, has appeared in Slavonic, Russian, German, English, French, and Italian. Nicodemos edited this great work and contributed numerous short biographies. The *Unseen Warfare* was revised and translated into Russian in the 19th century by Bishop Theophan the Recluse, and an English translation of this version appeared in England in 1952, with a valuable long Introduction by H. A. Hodges, Professor of Philosophy in the University of Reading.

Nicodemos' life, character, and thought have been dealt with at length in a book by Father Theocletos of the Monastery of Dionysiou that is entitled *Saint Nicodemos the Hagiorite* and was published in 1959.[59] More recently, a very uplifting akoluthia in honor of him was composed by the Athonite hymnographer Gerasimos of the Small Skete of St. Anne. The apolytikion of this akoluthia, which is chanted on July 14, says:

> "Being adorned with wisdom through Grace, O
> Father, thou hast appeared as a clarion of the
> Spirit emitting divine sounds, a teacher of the
> virtues, O God-inspired Nicodemos; for to all
> thou hast offered teachings for attaining salva-
> tion, purity of life, exhibiting mystical effulgence
> through the wealth of thy divine words, whereby
> thou hast given light unto the world."[60]

13. Bartholomew of Koutloumousiou

During the 19th century, the Holy Mountain produced very
few scholars. The main factors responsible for this were the following: (a) The occupation of the Mountain by 3,000 Turkish
soldiers during the Greek War of Independence (1821-1828), resulting in the departure of most of the monks — 5,000 out of 6,000
— and imposing upon the remaining monks the heavy burden of
feeding and paying this occupation army. (b) The confiscation of
the monasteries' landed estates in Moldavia and Wallachia. (c) The
extensive destruction by fire of nearly half the monasteries. And
(d) the growing influx into Greece of anti-monastic views from
Europe, views which have dominated an increasing number of
Greek politicians, intellectuals, and even clergymen.

There are two major scholars of this period: Bartholomew of
Koutloumousiou and Constantine Doukakis. Like Dapontes and
Nicodemos, Bartholomew (1772-1851) was a native of a small
Aegean island: Imvros, which is near the Dardenelles. After re-
ceiving a very elementary education in Imvros, he left for Athos.
Here he became a pupil of St. Nicodemos and also at the Athonias
Academy, receiving a good general education as well as instruction in
theology and philosophy.

Having been tonsured a monk in 1793 at the Monastery of
Koutloumousiou, he went to Kydoniai, on the west coast of Asia
Minor, for further studies at the renowned school of that city. When
he completed his education at Kydoniai, he returned to Athos.

Subsequently he spent many years as a teacher outside of
Athos. He taught first at Imvros, then at the school for priests in
Phanar (at Constantinople), at the Gymnasium in Halki, and at
the schools of Thessaloniki, Corfu, and Venice. During 1848-1849,
he taught at the Athonias Academy.

The chief publications of Bartholomew are a *Small Prayer
Book*,[61] for the use of students, a *Synopsis*[62] of prayers, designed for
all the Greeks and written at the exhortation of John Capodistrias,
the first ruler of liberated Greece, and corrected editions of the
following liturgical books of the Greek Church: the *Great Horologion*,[63] the *Pentekostarion*,[64] the *Triodion*,[65] and the twelve

Menaia.[66] A corrected edition of the liturgical books was much needed at that time, inasmuch as the repeated reprinting of them at foreign presses without comparing the text with older editions had resulted in the accumulation of countless errors. In correcting them, with the permission of four Patriarchs of Constantinople, Bartholomew had recourse to many printed editions and manuscripts found at Athos and elsewhere. Besides corrections, he contributed an Introduction to the *Pentekostarion* and one to the *Menaia,* both of them outstanding.

Bartholomew died in the Monastery of Koutloumousiou in 1851, at the age of eighty.

His earliest biographer, Manuel Gedeon, very aptly remarks: "The memory of his altruistic life lives and shall live forever, recommending to all the zeal, the piety, and the brotherly love of the scholar monks of the Holy Mountain."[67]

14. *Constantine Doukakis*

Constantine Doukakis (1845-1908) was born in Kalamata. From an early age he showed love of the monastic life, becoming a novice at the nearby Monastery of Velanidia after graduating from Kalamata's Gymnasium. At the age of twenty-nine he went to Mount Athos as a pilgrim and stayed there for two months. Upon his return to his native place, he bought an abandoned small monastery named after the prophet Elias and settled there after being tonsured a monk at the Monastery of Velanidia. Later he went to Athos twice in order to study various manuscripts and rare printed books in connection with the publications he was working on. He visited Athos a fourth time in 1904 and received the "Great and Angelic Habit," being renamed Cornelius.

His four sojourns at Athos, particularly the last, justify the inclusion of Doukakis among the Athonite monks. But he had another important link with the Holy Mountain: Father Alexios, a saintly confessor whom he had brought from the Mountain to his little monastery near Kalamata. Alexios helped make the monastery a significant center of spirituality.

In 1885, the Monastery of the Prophet Elias was destroyed by fire. This event marked the beginning of a new period in Doukakis'

life. He left for Athens and there undertook to bring about an extensive spiritual awakening of the Greeks by compiling and publishing edifying books. Thus, in 1885 he published a book entitled
Diamonds of Paradise,[68] containing discourses by the Fathers, and
commenced preparing a fourteen-volume collection of lives of
saints, called *Megas Synaxaristes*, "Great Book of the Lives of
Saints." The first twelve volumes of this work contain the lives of
saints of the twelve months of the year, while the other two volumes
contain those of the movable holy days included in the *Pentecostar-
ion* and the *Triodion*. He compiled it on the basis of many and
varied manuscripts and printed books, correcting the texts, amplify-
ing and clarifying them, translating them into the spoken language,
and adding the lives of recent martyrs and other saints. The publication of *Megas Synaxarites* began in 1889 and was completed in 1896.
A work great in magnitude and value, it superseded other works of
this type, and is to this day treasured in the monasteries of Greece
and read by pious people throughout that country.

Among the other publications of Doukakis are a second and
third edition of the book *On Continual Communion*[69] by Sts.
Macarios of Corinth and Nicodemos the Hagiorite, a new edition of
the *Leimonarion*[70] by John Moskos, and a *Pilgrim's Guide to the
Holy Mountain of Athos*.[71]

All his life Doukakis worked indefatigably for the spiritual
awakening and improvement of his fellow Christians, and thus acquired the reputation of being a very holy man.

15. *Gabriel, Abbot of Dionysiou*

In the 20th century, three remarkable writers have emerged
from Mount Athos. Two of them belong to the coenobitic Monastery
of Dionysiou: Archimandrite Gabriel and Father Theocletos. The
third, Vasilii (or Basil) Krivosheine, was for many years a monk at
the Monastery of Panteleimonos and is now Archbishop of Brussels
under the Patriarchate of Moscow.

Gabriel, who is considerably older than Theocletos, was born
in 1886 in the town of Mesenikolas near Karditsa, Thessaly. He was
educated at the schools of his native place. At the age of twenty-four
he left for the Holy Mountain and entered the Monastery of Diony-

siou. Having led an exemplary life here and displayed great talents, he was elected its abbot in 1936, following the death of the earlier abbot.

Since then, Father Gabriel has not only made this monastery one of the best in Greece, from the point of view of administration and spiritual life, but has done a great deal for elevating the morality and religious life of the people of Greece. Thus, he has been serving as confessor in many parts of Greece, delivering occasional lectures in Greek institutions of higher learning, contributing articles to newspapers and religious periodicals, and writing books. In addition, he has taken part in various meetings of Byzantinists.

He is the author of seven edifying books. His first book, *New Evergetinos*,[72] was published in 1950 and reprinted in 1954. It contains accounts of the Desert Fathers from the old *Evergetinos*[73] translated into the common Greek by George the Orator (18th century), and selected stories of recent ascetics. This book was followed by the *Lausaikon of the Holy Mountain*,[74] in which he deals with life and thought on Athos. He stresses the importance of Athonite monasticism and of Orthodox monasticism in general, remarking, for instance, that "monasticism was, is, and will continue to be the surest support of our Orthodoxy, of our Nation, of our Christian society."[75]

Subsequently he published *The Voice of One Crying from the Wilderness*,[76] *Malthusianism, or the Crime of Genocide*,[77] *Memories and Nostalgias*,[78] *The Holy Monastery of Saint Dionysiou*,[79] *The Monastic Life According to the Holy Fathers*,[80] and *Guide for the Confessor and the Confessant*.[81] The first contains twenty analytical and hortatory discourses dealing with various religious and social problems of Greece. It is one of his most penetrating and vigorous works. In the second he deals with the question of birth control and upholds the traditional Orthodox standpoint. *Memories and Nostalgias*, though autobiographical, seeks to arouse in the Greeks a better appreciation of all that is good and beautiful in the long history of their country. It was awarded First Prize in a literary contest organized by the Greek government. His book on Dionysiou is the first comprehensive work on this monastery, giving its history, describing its chapels and other buildings, its library, one of the

best organized on Athos, its collection of precious articles that are
of great historical and artistic interest, its rule, and in addition
sketching the lives of its saints and providing other pertinent in-
formation. *The Monastic Life* is a compilation of passages from
the Orthodox Church Fathers on the monastic life, grouped under
various headings, preceded by an illuminating prologue and closing
with valuable chapters on monasticism in Greece today. His *Guide*
is an important work, based on his long experience as a confessor
and on a careful study of Holy Scripture, the views of the Church
Fathers and Teachers, and the holy canons of the Ecumenical and
Local Synods.

In all his works Gabriel stresses the great importance of the
Church Fathers. He deplores the present tendency of many Greek
theologians and clerics to esteem highly the opinions of secular
savants, especially non-Greeks, and to ignore or slight the teachings
of the great luminaries of the Church, such as Sts. Basil the Great,
Gregory Nazianzen, John Chrysostom, and Symeon the New
Theologian.

16. *Theocletos of Dionysiou*

Father Theocletos, secretary and librarian of the Monastery of
Dionysiou, is the author of three good-sized books and of countless
articles that have appeared in religious journals between 1951 and
the present. Like his spiritual father, Gabriel, he occasionally makes
public appearances, addressing large audiences that are thirsting for
religious truth.

His first and most popular book, *Between Heaven and Earth*,[82]
was published in 1956 and again, in revised form, in 1967. Here is
presented in dialogue form a very eloquent and vigorous defense of
Athonite monasticism. This work displays not only wide learning,
but also remarkable dialectical ability, insight, and literary gifts.
It has made a profound impression upon people from all walks of
life in Greece and abroad. Father Theocletos vindicates the place
of contemplative, Athonite monasticism in the present age, and also
calls attention to the fact that asceticism or the regular use of bodily
and mental *askesis*, "training," is an essential characteristic of

authentic Orthodox Christianity. Thus he fully endorses the thesis of the Russian religious philosopher Nicholas Berdyaev that "Orthodoxy is more ascetic than Western Christianity, and is essentially a monastic religion."

The second book of Theocletos, *Saint Nicodemos the Hagiorite*,[83] is by far the most extensive account of the life and thought of this saint that has appeared in print. It is an extremely informative and edifying book.

Athonite Flowers[84] is the title of his third book. This consists of sixty-six articles that have appeared in various Greek religious publications, and are characterized by a strict adherence to, and defense of, the Orthodox Tradition that has been handed down by the Byzantines.

17. *Vasilii Krivosheine*

Born in Petersburg in 1900, Vasilii Krivosheine left Russia in 1920 and settled in Paris. In 1925 he went to Athos, and two years later he entered the Monastery of Panteleimonos. Here he mastered the Greek language and applied himself to the study of the Greek Church Fathers. A product of this study while he was still on Athos is the monograph *The Ascetic and Theological Teaching of Gregory Palamas*. This appeared in Russian in 1936,[85] and in English two years later.[86] He stayed on Athos until 1951, when he left for Oxford with the blessings of his monastery.

At Oxford he collaborated for five years in the preparation of the *Patristic Greek Lexicon* and also studied unpublished manuscripts of the writings of St. Symeon the New Theologian. His study of St. Symeon continued for many years in various libraries possessing such manuscripts, and resulted in a three-volume critical edition of thirty-four discourses of St. Symeon, entitled: *Symeon le Nouveau Theologien: Catecheses*.[87] This work includes, besides the Greek text, a French translation of it by Joseph Paramelle and introductions and notes in French written by Krivosheine.

He has written many articles in Russian, Greek, and English. Among those that have appeared in English are: "Mount Athos in the Spiritual Life of the Orthodox Church"[88] and "The Writings of St. Symeon the New Theologian."[89]

Since 1960, Vasilii has been Archbishop of Brussels and Belgium.

The appearance of Gabriel, Theocletos, and Krivosheine marks a significant revival of Orthodox mysticism on Mount Athos in the 20th century. Their deep interest in this mysticism is manifest from their great admiration of, and preoccupation with, mystical theologians such as Symeon, Palamas, and Nicodemos.

18. *Other Scholars*

Besides the scholars I have discussed, there have been numerous others who authored one or more works. Among the better known and more important of these are St. Dionysios the Orator, Theocletos and St. Hierotheos of Iviron, Procopios Dendrinos, Joachim Spetsieris, Theodosios of St. Paul's, Sofrony, and Theodoretos of the Skete of St. Anne.

Dionysios the Orator (d. 1606), the first settler of the Small Skete of St. Anne, was both a writer and an outstanding mystic who practiced and taught inner attention and mental prayer. He rendered into simple Greek many discourses of the Church Fathers which are concerned with the life of spiritual endeavor. A few of these have appeared in print.[90] The rest are preserved in manuscript form in various Athonite libraries. Thus, one of his manuscripts, bearing the title *Kouvaras*, is kept in the library of the Skete of St. Anne.

Theocletos of Iviron (fl. 1730) authored a dialogue entitled *The Cosmos and the Soul*,[91] while Hierotheos (1686-1745), of the same monastery, wrote a book against the heresy of the 17th century Spanish mystic Miguel de Molinos, and translated into modern Greek many discourses of St. Ephraim the Syrian and some lives of saints. These translations were published in the book *Discourses and Counsels of Our Holy Father Ephraim the Syrian together with Some Lives of Saints*.[92]

Procopios Dendrinos, who was born towards the end of the 18th century, perhaps in Ithaca, became a monk at the Russian Monastery of Panteleimonos. In 1830, the president of Greece, John Capodistrias, appointed him director of the school for training priests which was established that year in the island of Poros. Following the assissination of Capodistrias in 1831, Dendrinos went to Constantinople. Later he returned to Athos, where he died in 1848. He authored four small doctrinal treatises, which were published between 1831 and 1841. These are: *Guide, or Introduction to the Divine Scriptures*,[93] *Manual, or Study Against Those Who are Opposed to the Veneration of the Theotokos and the Holy Cross*,[94] *Refutation of the Booklet Against the Origin of Ancestral Sin*,[95] and *Christian Teaching, or Catechism*.[96]

For many years a hermit at the New Skete, Archimandrite Joachim Spetsieris (1858-1943) authored besides other works a very popular book on *The Hermitess Photine*,[97] and the life of St. Nectarios Kephalas, Metropolitan of Pentapolis. The latter has been translated into English.[98]

Theodosios was for over a decade editor of the periodical *St. Paul of Xeropotamou*,[99] which was published by the Monastery of St. Paul, of which he has been for a long time librarian. He has authored a significant book dealing with the subject of Holy Communion.[100]

Archimandrite Sofrony, who was a disciple of the Russian monk Silouan (1866-1938) of the Monastery of Panteleimonos and now leads a monastic life in Essex England, has authored a remarkable book, entitled *The Undistorted Image: Staretz Silouan*.[101] In this book, which first appeared in Russian and later in English, Sofrony presents the life and teaching of his spiritual guide.

Finally, the young monk Theodoretos of the Skete of St. Anne has written two notable books: *Saint Nectarios: The Hierarch, the Scholar, the Ascetic*,[102] and *Dialogues of the Desert on Ecumenism*.[103] The first is a scholarly treatment of St. Nectarios Kephalas, while the second is a discussion of the contemporary "Ecumenical" movement from the canonical, Orthodox standpoint.

Many other religious writers, who cannot be designated as Athonites, dwelt on Mount Athos for years and benefited immensely from their stay there. Among these are the renowned theologian Metrophanis Kritopoulos (1589-1639), Patriarch of Alexandria;[104] the Great Educators of the Greek Nation of the 18th century Eugene Voulgaris,[105] St. Macarios of Corinth,[106] and Athanasios

Parios;[107] and St. Gregory V, Patriarch of Constantinople.[108] Furthermore, countless have been the learned men who have been profoundly influenced by visits of months or weeks to the Holy Mountain. Among the Greeks, I might cite the late Fotis Kontoglou, outstanding literary and religious writer and icon painter;[109] among the Russians, Constantine N. Leontiev, eminent thinker and writer of the last century.[110]

CHAPTER II

MISSIONARIES

Having spoken of the scholars of the Holy Mountain, I turn now to its missionaries. I have much less to say under this heading, partly because there have been relatively few Athonite missionaries in the narrower sense of the term, and partly because several of the scholars I have discussed were also missionaries, and I have noted their missionary activities — e.g. Maximos the Greek, Agapios Landos, and Dionysios of Fourna. Taking the term Athonite missionaries in the narrower sense, to denote those who have gone beyond the borders of the Mountain and sought to enlighten and regenerate their fellow men by preaching and counseling, I note the following missionaries not discussed thus far: Antony Pechersky the Russian, Sava of Serbia, Niphon and his disciples Macarios and Joasaph of the Monastery of Dionysiou, Nil Sorsky the Russian, Iakovos of Iviron, Damian, Symeon and Cosmas Aitolos of Philotheou, and Cyprian of Koutloumousiou. All of them are recognized as saints. Six are martyrs — Macarios, Joasaph, Iakovos, Damian, Cosmas and Cyprian — having been put to death by the Turks for publicly professing and teaching the Christian faith.

1. St. Antony Pechersky

The first outstanding missionary was St. Antony Pechersky (d. 1073), one of the earliest Russian saints and, together with his disciple Theodosius, the founder of the first great Russian monastery, the Pecherskaya Lavra or "Cave Monastery" near Kiev. From his biographer Nestor, the first Russian historiographer, who became a monk at this monastery, we learn, among other things pertaining to St. Antony, the following:

Having renounced the world, Antony went to Athos, where he received the Great and Angelic Habit at the Monastery of Esphigmenou by its abbot Theoktistos. At Esphigmenou he learned "the art of arts and the science of sciences" — the monastic way — and led an exemplary life of obedience and spiritual endeavor. Following a vision, Theoktistos instructed him to go back to Russia and transmit Athonite monasticism to the Russian people, and thus become the father of regular monasticism in that country. Antony went there but did not stay very long, as a persecution of virtuous and holy men was undertaken by a new, tyrannical ruler. He returned to Athos. Longing for greater stillness than was possible in a monastery, he asked for and received the consent of the abbot of Esphigmenou to go and live alone on a nearby mountain. When another, pious ruler came into power in Russia, Theoktistos again saw a vision in which he was told to send Antony to that country. So he exhorted Antony to go and complete his mission in Russia, establishing monasteries as "schools of virtue" leading to salvation. Accordingly, St. Antony went to Kiev, established a hermitage in a cave near that city, and began attracting devout disciples, teaching them the lofty monastic ideals and methods, which he had not only learned but also lived on the Holy Mountain.

As more and more disciples gathered about him, he and his most gifted disciple, St. Theodosius, founded the great Pechersk Monastery of Kiev, then capital of Russia. This monastery became the model for numerous other monasteries that were subsequently established in Russia. Antony died here on July 10, 1073, at the age of ninety.

He is commemorated on July 10, and this couplet is recited by the Greek Orthodox in his honor:

"Antony, the leader of the chorus of monastics in Russia,
Made known an incorporeal way of life."

On Athos there is a chapel in the environs of the Monastery of Esphigmenou dedicated to St. Antony Pechersky; and a mural icon of him is to be seen in the outer narthex of Esphigmenou's main church.

2. *St. Sava of Serbia*

A century after the repose of St. Antony Pechersky, there appeared on Athos two other great figures, Sava and his father Symeon. During their worldly life their names were Rastko and Stephen Nemanya. Before he became a monk Stephen (1113-1199) was the mighty ruler of Serbia who succeeded in uniting the scattered Serbian clans into one nation, while Rastko (1169-1235) was the youngest of his three sons. As a youth Rastko was noted for his intelligence, kindness, purity, and meditativeness.

Prince Rastko embraced the monastic life years before his father. At the age of seventeen, as his parents were about to wed him, he fled secretly to Mount Athos and entered the Russian monastery. He was tonsured a monk here and given the name Sava only a few days after his arrival, in order to make it impossible for the officers, whom his father had sent, to take him forcibly back to the palace.

His decision to go to the Holy Mountain was the result of his realization that worldly kingdoms, riches, glory and luxury are transitory and do not satisfy man's deeper self; and that man's supreme goal should be to attain illumination and the blessedness of the kingdom of God that is within us.

After several months at the Russian monastery, Sava went to the Monastery of Vatopedi. Here he spent the next twelve years, occupying himself with prayer, his appointed chores, and study. Having mastered the Greek language, he conversed with the hermits of Athos, whom he greatly admired, and learned from them the art of mental prayer. Also, he studied avidly the writings of the Greek Church Fathers which he found in the library of Vatopedi.

His parents repeatedly pleaded to him through letters to return to them. But in vain. Not only would he not go back, but he exhorted them to give up royalty and the world, and adopt the monastic life. Finally they heeded his exhortations. In 1196 Stephen Nemanya abdicated his throne and took monastic vows at the Monastery of Studenitza, in Serbia, which he had founded in 1183, while his wife, Anna, became a nun at the Convent of the Holy

Virgin, also in Serbia. Stephen's name was now changed to Symeon and that of Anna to Anastasia.

Symeon lived at Studenitza for a year and a half as a simple monk, and then left for the Holy Mountain, to spend the rest of his days there. He entered Vatopedi, where Sava was. Here he became an exemplary monk, leading as austere a life of spiritual striving as his age permitted, practicing unceasing prayer. After two years he founded, together with Sava, the Monastery of Hilandari, also known as the Serbian Monastery, which survives to this day. He died here on February 13, 1199 — the year it was founded — at the age of eighty-six.

After his father's death, aspiring to rise higher on the ladder of spiritual perfection, Sava retired to a hermitage, a "house of stillness" (*hesychasterion*), in Karyes, and emulated the great ascetic-mystical Fathers of the Eastern Church in their fasts, kneelings, and other physical practices, as well as in mental practices such as meditation and unceasing interior prayer. Thus he gained illumination and peace of soul beyond understanding.

Having dwelt on the Holy Mountain for twenty years, St. Sava left for Serbia. The purpose of his return was twofold: to bring the relics of his father as a sacred treasure to the Serbs, and to reconcile his brothers Stephen and Vukan, who were in serious conflict about the sovereignty of their country, which Symeon had entrusted to Stephen. Sava intended to return to Athos as soon as this reconciliation had been effected. However, having enshrined the relics of St. Symeon in the Monastery of Studenitza, and united his brothers in love, he did not leave for Athos as he had planned. His return to his beloved house of stillness was to materialize much later, and then only for a period of two years. Seeing the lamentable spiritual state of his fellow countrymen, he settled at Studenitza and undertook the great mission of transforming the Serbs into a holy nation. To this end he trained monks for missionary work and others for parish priesthood. He himself preached to, and counseled, the pilgrims who came to the monastery in large numbers to see him and to venerate the sacred relics of Symeon; and from time to time he traveled among the people to instruct them in the true faith and help bring about their regeneration.

St. Sava firmly believed that Orthodoxy is the only true way of salvation. And seeing that two formidable forces were contending in Serbia against it: the heresy of the Bogomils on the one hand and Roman Catholicism on the other, he sought to organize the Orthodox Church there into a more efficient religious body, capable of protecting its members from proselytism and of winning back those who had gone astray. One very important step for achieving this was, he believed, to secure the autonomy of the Serbian Church, which till then was subject to the Archbishopric of Ochrida in Epiros, part of the Byzantine Empire. Hence he went to Nicaea, Asia Minor, where the Byzantine Emperor and the Patriarch of Constantinople dwelt after the Crusaders seized the imperial city of Constantinople, and explained his case to them. Having listened to his very moving presentation, they granted autonomy to the Serbian Church. And considering Sava the ideal person to become the leader of that Church, they persuaded him — after his insistent protests that he was unworthy — to accept their nomination. He was ordained in 1219 at Nicaea by the Patriarch Manuel I assisted by the Greek bishops, in the presence of Emperor Theodore Laskaris, becoming the first Archbishop of the independent Serbian Church.

Sava Nemanya was not only a great ascetic and apostle of the Orthodox Faith, but also the first Serbian scholar. He wrote the rules of the monasteries of Hilandari and Studenitza, and *The Life of Saint Symeon,* giving an account of the life of his father. This book is one of the best works in Serbian literature.

He died on January 14, 1235, in the Bulgarian city of Tirnovo, where he was staying as a guest after a long pilgrimage during which he visited Mount Athos, the Holy Land, the regions of Egypt where the Desert Fathers had dwelt, and the Monastery of St. Catherine on Mount Sinai.

The earliest life of St. Sava was written by his disciple Arseny, who succeeded him in 1233 as Archbishop of Serbia. Many miraculous cures are attributed to Sava as well as to Symeon.

Sava is regarded by the Serbs as their greatest saint. The very high esteem in which he is held by them is testified by the fact that there are numerous icons depicting him, and many churches in his name. Thus, over twenty mural icons of Sava are preserved in the Serbian monasteries, including Hilandari, while in the United States alone there are seven churches and a monastery dedicated to him.

Bishop Nicholai Velimerovich of the Serbian Orthodox Church of America gives an extensive account of the life of St. Sava in his book *The Life of St. Sava.*[1]

On January 12, when he is commemorated, the Orthodox chant the following apolytikion:

> "Thou wast a guide of the way that leadeth to life, and a first prelate and teacher. For thou didst come and enlighten thy home country, O Saint Sava, having given it rebirth by the Holy Spirit. Thou didst plant thy holy children like olive trees in the spiritual paradise. Wherefore, honoring thee as a peer of the Apostles and Saints, we implore: Pray to Christ our God to grant us great mercy."

3. *St. Niphon, Patriarch of Constantinople*

Niphon (*c.* 1425-1515) was born in the Peloponnesos, and hence is known as the Peloponnesian. He received his education from three learned monks and was tonsured by one of them, named Antony, at Epidaurus. After the death of Antony he went to the castle of Narda, where he met a very devout Athonite monk, Zacharias. Together with him, Niphon went and settled at the Monastery of the Theotokos in Ochrida. When Zacharias became Archbishop of Ochrida, he took Niphon with him in an extensive mission throughout Greece as well as Dalmatia and Illyricum. The purpose of this mission was to condemn publicly the decrees of the Synod of Florence (1438-1439) — decrees which constituted a surrender of the Orthodox Church to the claims of the Papacy — and in general to instruct the Christians in the true doctrines and to strengthen them in the Orthodox faith.

After his mission Niphon went to the Holy Mountain, where

he stayed for brief periods at the monasteries of Vatopedi and Pantocratoros, and then entered the Monastery of Dionysiou. Here he was ordained deacon and later priest. Subsequently, he was made successively Metropolitan of Thessaloniki and Patriarch of Constantinople. His tenure as Patriarch was interrupted twice, owing to the intrigues of the Greeks of his diocese and the interventions of the Turks. He was Patriarch from 1486 to 1489, and from 1497 to 1498.

Following his second withdrawal from the Patriarchate he went to Wallachia, at the invitation of the ruler of that country, Radoulos I, the Great, to preach to the people. He offered great services to the Christians there. In his akoluthia in honor of this saint, Nicodemos the Hagiorite says that Niphon "enlightened that country and adorned it with Christian practices and virtues, whereas previously it was full of wickedness."[2] And in his brief biography of Niphon, which is contained in his book *The Holy Monastery of Saint Dionysiou,* Archimandrite Gabriel remarks that through his holy life, his instruction and exhortations in Wallachia, St. Niphon saved Orthodoxy there from Papism, which via Uniatism had penetrated far into the northern provinces of Transylvania and Galicia.

After an absence of forty years, Niphon returned to the Monastery of Dionysiou. He died there in 1515, at the age of ninety. The Orthodox commemorate him on August 11, chanting many beautiful hymns in his honor, such as the following one:

> "By godly deeds hast thou shone forth; thou hast
> illumined the whole Church, being exalted in
> the ways of humility; for having been glorified
> on Athos through spiritual striving, thou hast re-
> ceived the name adornment of Patriarchs. O glori-
> ous Niphon, fill with divine graces those who
> with faith and aspiration magnify thee."

An excellent account of his life has been written by Nicodemos the Hagiorite and has recently appeared in English.[3]

4. St. Macarios of Dionysiou

About Macarios and Joasaph much less is known than about their master Niphon. In the *New Martyrologium* of Sts. Macarios and Nicodemos, and in Archimandrite Gabriel's book on the Monastery of Dionysiou, we find the following essential data about Macarios.

He was a disciple of St. Niphon. Being a great spiritual striver according to Christ, a keeper of strictness in the monastic life and in all things an emulator of the virtues of his teacher, he aspired to go out into the world and preach, to strengthen the Christians in the faith and bring back to the faith those who had denied it. So he revealed this longing to Niphon, received his blessings and left for Thessaloniki. Macarios' preaching resulted in his being seized by the Turks, imprisoned, and beheaded on September 14, 1507.

The following verses by Nicodemos the Hagiorite are recited on the anniversary of his martyrdom:

"Thou art blessed, O Macarios, and through martyrdom
Thou didst go away to the realm of the blessed."

5. St. Joasaph of Dionysiou

About Joasaph we learn from the same sources the following. He was an emulator of the excellences of his teacher Niphon, and served him faithfully until the latter's death. Before Niphon died, Joasaph had expressed to him the eager desire to go out and preach, and received his master's consent and blessings. In 1516, he went to Constantinople and preached the Christian faith in the presence of the Turks. As in the case of Macarios, this resulted in his being arrested by them, tortured and beheaded. He died on October 26, 1518.

These verses are recited on October 26 in commemoration of his life as a monk and martyr:

"Having joined spiritual striving with trial, O all-
blissful one,
Thou receivest a double crown, O Joasaph."

6. *St. Nil Sorsky*

St. Nil(os) Sorsky (*c.* 1433-1508), who is of great importance in Russian monasticism, was in his prime about four centuries after the death of St. Antony Pechersky, the first introducer of Athonite monasticism into Russia. The son of Russian peasants, Nil received his education in monasteries, studying the main literature then available in Russia: the lives of martyrs and other saints. Monasticism attracted him, and he became a monk in his youth at the famous monastery of Belozersk, which had been founded by St. Cyril (1337-1427). This monastery had one of the best libraries in Russia, containing among other works Slavonic translations of Greek Patristic writings made by the monks of Athos.

After some time at this monastery, Nil went on a pilgrimage to the Holy Mountain, accompanied by his friend St. Innocent of Okhlyabinin. This pilgrimage turned into a sojourn of several years, during which he not only visited the monasteries and hermitages of the Mountain, but also read extensively books on prayer and mysticism, either in the original Greek language, which he appears to have mastered here, or in Russian translation. About this sojourn he afterward remarked: "I lived like a bee flitting from one fine flower to another, in order to know the garden of life and of Christian truth, and in order to revive my flagging soul and to prepare it for salvation."[4] From books and from spiritual guides on Athos he learned the theory and practice of mental prayer.

Having become a possessor of deep theological knowledge as well as a spiritual man, a mystic, Nil made it his special mission in life, upon returning to his native land, to teach the spiritual ideas and practices of Athonite monasticism. Of the various forms of monastic life on the Holy Mountain, he liked best that led by hermits at the sketes. So he introduced this form of monasticism into Russia. He built a hut in the wilderness about ten miles from Belozersk and withdrew there. Disciples settled near him, and thus the first skete in Russia was formed.

At this skete Nil and his disciples collaborated in copying, translating and studying Greek ascetical and mystical writings, extracting from them those elements which they needed for their own spiritual development as well as that of their fellow countrymen. Out of this painstaking work there resulted a whole system of spiritual teaching, which he excellently summed up in two major works: *Tradition to the Disciples* and *Monastic Rule*. The first consists of letters addressed to his disciples, while the second is a long treatise in eleven chapters. In them he summarizes, for the first time in Russia, the teaching of the Orthodox ascetic-mystical Fathers, such as Sts. Basil, John Climacos, Barsanuphios, Abba Dorotheos, Symeon the New Theologian, and Gregory the Sinaite. G. P. Fedotov has included selections from these works in his *Treasury of Russian Spirituality*.[5]

The apolytikion which is chanted in honor of St. Nil on May 7 calls attention to his work as a gatherer of precious teachings from such Fathers:

> "Having renounced the world, and fleeing the
> tumult of this life, O righteous and God-bearing
> Father Nilos, thou didst not neglect to gather
> paradisiacal flowers from the writings of the
> Fathers. Having settled in the wilderness, from
> whence thou didst pass into heavenly mansions,
> thou didst blossom as a lily of the field. Where-
> fore, teach us, who venerate thee with honor, to
> walk by thy royal way, and do thou pray for our
> souls."

St. Nil explains in his works important interior practices, such as guarding of the mind, spiritual combat, meditation, concentration, and mental prayer, and also numerous other matters pertaining to the spiritual life. With regard to mental prayer, it should be noted that he was the first to bring to Russia the theory of mental prayer from Athos. Whereas the tendency in contemporary Russian monasticism was to concern itself with external discipline and mechanical ritual, and to become deeply involved in worldly affairs, Nil stressed that the essence of monasticism is the interior, spiritual life.

In his time Russian monasticism had not only neglected the

interior life, but had turned into a system of exploiting the peasants, degrading them to serfs. The monasteries had acquired vast estates, including entire villages, and used their inhabitants as merely means for the prosperity of the monks. Having learned the nature of true monasticism on Athos, the holy father condemned this aberrant form of Russian monasticism. He taught that monasteries should not possess villages and use the peasants as serfs; that monks should live in poverty and by the work of their own hands. Christianity, he pointed out, is a religion of the spirit, of freedom, and of love; and hence the monks should seek to acquire inner, not outer wealth, and to put in order the inner man, not to manage great landed estates, exploiting and degrading their fellow men. The saint considered the latter preoccupation as poison for monasticism, inasmuch as it causes the monks to become entangled in worldly concerns and forget their spiritual vocation. Nil saw the sketic form of the monastic life as the solution to the problem of the secularization of monasticism.

He declared his views on this matter formally in the council that met in Moscow in 1503. Made up of bishops and monks who came from wealthy monasteries, the council rejected his ideas for reform. Hence the evils which he sought to eliminate continued, and they were noted by Maximos the Greek when he came to Russia in 1518, ten years after Nil's death. Maximos, too, as I noted earlier, sought to reform Russian monasticism, to bring it back to the true path.

The importance of St. Nil Sorsky for Russian spirituality and his close relationship to Athos have been increasingly recognized in our time. One notes this, for example, in a chapter devoted to him by Constantin de Grunwald in his book *Saints of Russia,*[6] and one by G. P. Fedotov in *The Russian Religious Mind,*[7] as well as in Fedotov's Introduction to the selections from St. Nil contained in *Treasury of Russian Spirituality.*

7. St. Iakovos of Iviron

An account of the life of St. Iakovos of Iviron is contained in *New Martyrologium.* He was a native of a village near Kastoria, in northern Greece. At an early age he went to Constantinople. There he became very wealthy. But having learned of the great holiness of Niphon, who was the Patriarch at that city, met him and confessed to him, Iakovos gave away his wealth to the poor and went to the Holy Mountain. After visiting the monasteries there, he entered that of Docheiariou. Later he withdrew to the Skete of Prodromou, a dependency of the Monastery of Iviron. Leading a very austere life of spiritual endeavor at this skete, he experienced divine illumination, acquired the gifts of prophecy and of knowing men's hidden thoughts, and became a spiritual teacher and guide known throughout Athos.

When the idea came to him of going outside of Athos to edify his fellow Christians, and he became convinced that it was the will of God that he do so, he took two of his disciples — Iakovos the Deacon and Dionysios — and went to various parts of Greece. Beginning from Thessaloniki, he visited among other places the Meteora in Thessaly, and went as far south as Naupaktos, across from Patras. At the Meteora, the monasteries which are built on the tops of enormous rocks, he corrected the monks. At Naupaktos, he settled in the Monastery of Prodromou and preached to large crowds that came down from the surrounding regions to listen to his edifying teaching.

Unfortunately, the bishop of Arta, fearing that certain unlawful acts of his might be brought to the light by this extraordinary monk, slandered him to the Turkish authorities, saying that he was preparing a rebellion against them. As a result, Iakovos and his two disciples were seized by the Turks and brought to the Sultan at Adrianople. After being cruelly tortured for seventeen days, all three were hanged. The date of their martyrdom was November 1, 1520.

The following apolytikion, contained in the akoluthia in honor of him and his two disciples, is chanted on November 1st:

      "Having led an eminently angelic life on earth,
        thou didst receive the gift of the Apostles; and
        having been sent as a teacher of repentance, thou
        didst show, to those who wished, the path of
        salvation; wherefore also thou didst stand up at

the trial bravely, together with thy firm fellow
strivers, O wise and holy Iakovos the exceedingly great."

8. *St. Damian of Philotheou*

Another martyr missionary of the 16th century, Damian of the
Monastery of Philotheou, was a native of the village of Richovon
(or Merichovon), near Agrapha. At an early age he went to Athos
and was tonsured a monk at the Monastery of Philotheou. After
some time there, he withdrew to a hermitage, becoming a disciple
of an elder named Dometios. When he had stayed here for three
years, he heard a supernatural voice urging him to go out and
teach. He obeyed it and went and preached in many regions of
Greece, including those of Olympos, Kissavos, Larissa, and Agrapha.

In the *New Martyrologium* we read: "He preached the word
of God eloquently, teaching and exhorting the Christians to repent
and abstain from injustices and all other vices, and to keep the
commandments of God, doing good and God-pleasing works."[8]

At Kissavos, besides preaching he built a monastery, where
he led a life of daily prayer together with other monks. "Many
people went there," we read in the same book, "in order to benefit
spiritually by his edifying teaching, for he was a very sagacious man
and full of Divine gifts."[9]

In February, 1568, while on his way to a village, Damian was
arrested by the Turks and cast into prison. He was hanged and then
thrown into a fire on February 23, after having been subjected to
great tortures for fifteen days.

Nicodemos penned the following verses in commemoration of
this missionary:

"Thou hast received the fruit of the Gospel,
O Blessed Damian, through death by hanging."

9. *St. Symeon of Philotheou*

Symeon of the Monastery of Philotheou was born around 1500

in a village near Larissa. He dwelt for years on Athos and became abbot of Philotheou. Later he went and preached to the people in the regions of Zagora, Larissa, Evrippos, and Athens. Subsequently, he withdrew to the mountain Phlamourion in Zagora, Thessaly, built a monastery dedicated to the Holy Trinity, and there led a life of spiritual endeavor together with some other monks.

The memory of Symeon is celebrated on April 19. His akoluthia, which was written by the hiermonk Germanos and published in Smyrna in 1764, contains, among many other beautiful hymns, the following kontakion:

> "Having come to have thy being wholly in God,
> O Holy one, and having become through the virtues bright like the sun, O Father, thou hast flashed forth in miracles and illuminated the world by means of signs and teachings. Wherefore thou didst become by thy nature an excellent trainer of monastics. Hence we cry out: Rejoice, O thrice-blessed Father."

10. *St. Cyprian of Koutloumousiou*

Cyprian, a native of Agrapha, became a monk and priest at the Monastery of Koutloumousiou. Leaving the Holy Mountain, he went to Thessaloniki and Constantinople, and there preached the Christian faith and censured the unbelief of the Turks. This resulted in his being arrested by the Turks, tortured and beheaded. He suffered martyrdom on July 5, 1679, at Constantinople.

Nicodemos the Hagiorite wrote these verses in commemoration of Cyprian's martyrdom:

> "Cyprian, burning with spiritual love,
> Regarded the tortures altogether as luxuries."

11. *St. Cosmas Aitolos*

The greatest martyr missionary that came out of the Holy Mountain is St. Cosmas Aitolos (1714-1779). Cosmas was born in the village of Mega Dendron of Aitolia, near Naupaktos. He attended schools in Aitolia and then Athos' school of higher learning, the Athonias Academy. Upon leaving the Academy, he went to the Monastery of Philotheou, where he was tonsured a monk and later was ordained priest. He stayed here for seventeen years, fulfilling conscientiously his duties as the priest of the monastery, striving to perfect the inner man, and enriching his knowledge of religion by assiduous study. According to his own confession, he devoted over forty years of his life to study, as a result of which he came to the conclusion that Orthodoxy is the only true faith.

While at the monastery, Cosmas felt called by God to undertake the mission of enlightening and regenerating his fellow Christians. The Greeks, he was keenly aware, had fallen into great ignorance as regards their religion, and this was not only resulting in many forms of wickedness, but also in large numbers of them abandoning Orthodoxy and embracing Islam. Therefore he sought and obtained the consent of his elders to undertake such a mission. Leaving the Holy Mountain, he went to Constantinople, met the Patriarch Seraphim (1757-1761), and obtained from him a written permit to preach throughout the Greek world. This was necessary for him in order to avoid hindrance from the Turkish authorities and local bishops.

Cosmas' mission commenced in 1760, when he was forty-six years old, and continued, with a few interruptions, until the time of his martyrdom at the hands of the Turks in 1779. His missionary activities and their impact have been described at length by his learned disciple Sapphiros Christodoulidis, in his life of the great missionary contained in the *New Martyrologium*.[10] From this we learn that Cosmas preached in Constantinople and its suburbs, Thessaloniki, Verroia, Mount Athos and nearly all the rest of Macedonia, throughout the Greek mainland south of Macedonia as far as Messolonghi and Naupaktos, in Albania, in the Ionian and Dodecanese Islands.

He addressed large audiences, explaining to them the basic doctrines of Eastern Orthodoxy, dissuading people from wickedness, exhorting them to lead a godly life, stressing the need of instruction in the true faith, and establishing schools in many towns and villages. From one of his letters, written shortly before his martyrdom, we learn that he established two hundred "common" or elementary schools and ten "Greek" or higher schools. Cosmas believed that churches are of little value without schools where thorough religious instruction is offered.

Assigning great value to edifying publications, the Saint gave away catechisms and books by the Greek Church Fathers, which he persuaded the well-to-do to give him for free distribution.

The missionary activities of Cosmas were exceedingly effective. "Wherever this thrice-blessed man went," says Christodoulidis, "people listened with great contrition and devoutness to his grace-imbued and sweet words, and there resulted great improvement in their ways and great benefit to their souls. . . . Aided by Divine grace, he tamed the fierce, rendered brigands gentle, made the pitiless and unmerciful compassionate and merciful, the impious pious, instructed those who were ignorant in divine things and made them attend the church services, and briefly he brought the sinners to great repentance and correction, so that everybody was saying that in our times there has appeared a new Apostle."[11]

Not only the Christians, but Moslems also regarded Cosmas Aitolos as a saint, because of his inspiring sermons, his impeccable character, and the miraculous events which occurred at many places that he visited. The Greeks have named him *Isapostolos,* a "Peer of the Apostles." And he may rightly be called the father of modern Greece, inasmuch as he played a role of supreme importance in the ethico-religious awakening and enlightenment of the Greeks during the second half of the 18th century, and thus more than anyone else inaugurated the modern Greek era.

Many books and numerous articles about St. Cosmas have been published in Greece. They are listed in Kostas Sardelis' *Analytic Bibliography of Cosmas Aitolos.*[12] Here in America, a volume giving an account of the life, character and message of the saint, together with selections from his *Didachai,* "Teachings," has recently appeared in English.[13]

The akoluthia which is chanted in his honor on August 24 contains the following characteristic hymn, his kontakion:

> "Having come from Aitolia, O God-inspired Father, and led the life of a monk on Athos, and been truly initiated into the glory of God, thou didst proclaim to all the word of truth, and lead all to Christ, O most-blessed one, emulator of the Apostles, who didst become a holy martyr by shedding thy blood."

12. *Other Missionaries*

There have undoubtedly been many other missionaries, whose lives have not been recorded. Thus, the Monastery of Iviron is known to have had a long tradition of missionary activity, which continues down to the present, though little is known about its particular missionaries. In his *Lausaikon of the Holy Mountain,* Archimandrite Gabriel of Dionysiou says: "The Monastery of Iviron has for centuries spread its fragrance to Orthodox countries as far as the Caucasus and Russia. From this monastery there used to be sent as missionaries to those remote countries virtuous and venerable fathers, full of love and self-denial, fathers who were faithful keepers of the injunctions of St. Paul, according to which 'there is neither Greek nor barbarian, but Christ is all and in all.' Serving abroad in that spirit, they strengthened souls and brought glory to their fellow-countrymen. . . . From this monastery one will meet spiritual sons in the remotest parts of the world, serving the spiritual needs of their fellow-religionists, and spreading the light of Orthodoxy among others. . . . Father Agathangelos in Cairo, where he died recently, Aimilianos in America, Pangratios in Thessaloniki, and others in South Africa and Australia became founders of important centers of spiritual and sanctifying activity."[14]

CHAPTER III

SAINTS

In speaking of the scholars and missionaries of the Holy Mountain, I have already dealt with a good number of its saints. It remains for me to say something about the concept of a saint, to give an idea of the number of saints of Athos, to dwell somewhat on those not yet discussed that have been especially significant, and to say a few words about their way of life.

What is a saint? According to the teaching of the Orthodox Church Fathers, a saint is a person who has become a partaker of Divine grace, is guided and inspired by the Holy Spirit. Such a person is free from every vice and the possessor of all the virtues. "The mark of the saints," Basil the Great tells us, "is their life according to God, their divine conduct." Saints are distinguished into different orders, according to their special gifts or the different circumstances of their lives. There are Prophets, Apostles, Martyrs, Confessors, Teachers, Ascetics, and the Righteous. These are not mutually exclusive categories: a particular saint may belong to several of these categories. Among the saints of the Holy Mountain all of these orders are represented.

Saints have been attributed to nearly all the monasteries, but especially to Lavra, Vatopedi, Iviron, Dionysiou, and Zographou. About ninety were tonsured and dwelt in these monasteries or their dependencies, i.e. sketes, kellia, or hermitages. The most complete enumeration of the saints of the Mountain is contained in the revised akoluthia in honor of all the Athonite saints that was prepared and published there in 1941 by the hiermonk Daniel and the monk Nectarios. Its title is *Akoluthia of Our Holy and God-inspired Fathers Who Shone on the Holy Mountain of Athos*.[1] The service is chanted on the Sunday after the Sunday of all Saints. But

60

even this work does not mention all the Hagiorite saints. I have found some additional ones in the *Hagiology of the Orthodox Church* by Sophronios Eustratiadis[2] and in some other books. Altogether one hundred and thirty saints of Athos are mentioned in these works, plus an unspecified number of 13th century martyrs of certain monasteries. The latter were put to death because they censured the Byzantine emperor Michael Palaiologos and the Patriarch of Constantinople John Bekkos for seeking to unite the Orthodox Church with the Roman Catholic. Eustratiadis and other writers who mention the Hagiorite monks who suffered martyrdom on that occasion give definite numbers only in the case of the monasteries of Zographou and Vatopedi. Zographou, the Bulgarian monastery, is credited with twenty-six such martyrs; Vatopedi, with twelve.

1. *Martyrs*

About half of the saints of the Holy Mountain are martyrs. The martyrs of the Byzantine period were put to death by the Latinizing faction of Palaiologos and Bekkos, while those of the post-Byzantine period were executed by the Turks. Concerning the martyrdom of the twenty-six monks of Zographou, Eustratiadis says this:

"Among the Hagiorite fathers who were persecuted and found bitter death by the Latinizing king Michael Palaiologos (1261-1282) and John Bekkos (1275-1282) are included twenty-six monks of the Monastery of Zographou. Abiding steadfastly by the dogmas of the Fathers, these monks by no means yielded to the royal commands, but fearlessly censured those who accepted the doctrines of the Latins. . . . According to the account that has been handed down, the monks of Zographou shut themselves up in the monastery and from the tower censured the Latinizers, calling them lawless and heretics. The latter lighted a fire and burned to death the twenty-six monks."[3]

About the twelve martyrs of Vatopedi, Eustratiadis says: "These, having censured the Latinizing Michael Palaiologos and John Bekkos for having gone astray, were subjected, together with the abbot of the monastery, Euthymios, to martyrdom."[4]

The circumstances of martyrdom in the period of Turkish Rule were varied. We have already noted one of them: the fact that the monk went into the world and preached. Other monks suffered martyrdom because, while outside of Athos for some matter that pertained to their monastery, they were falsely accused of serious misbehavior towards some Turk. Following the accusation, they were tortured and urged to renounce Christianity and embrace Islam, but as they refused to do this they were put to death. The story of many a martyr runs as follows. As a child he was brought up in the Orthodox faith. At an early age he was forced to embrace Islam. Later he broke away from Islam and went to the Holy Mountain, confessed his sin, became a monk, and led a life of spiritual endeavor. Finally, to wipe out the stain of apostasy, he left the Mountain and professed his Christian faith before the Turks, denouncing Islam as a counterfeit religion. This resulted in his being tortured and executed.

The lives of the martyrs of the Holy Mountain have been of great significance for Orthodox Christendom, stressing the supreme importance (a) of true belief in matters of religion and (b) of openly professing such belief. Orthodoxy, it should be remembered, means precisely true belief. These martyrs regarded false religious belief as resulting in separation from God, and separation from God as being spiritual death, hell.

2. *Teachers and Ascetics*

Two other major categories of Athonite saints are the Teachers and the Ascetics. I have already dealt with the Teacher saints in discussing the scholars, a scholar saint being in the terminology of Orthodox hagiology a Teacher. The noun *ascetic* means *spiritual striver,* one who disciplines himself with a view to spiritual perfection. In this sense all the Athonite saints were ascetics, having led a life of incessant spiritual endeavor. But I am using the term Ascetic, for want of a better one, to denote those saints who in Greek Orthodox writings are called *Hosioi,* which means literally saints or holy men, but in a narrower sense denotes those monastic saints who did not suffer martyrdom and who distinguished themselves primarily for their holy life as spiritual strivers. The Ascetics are, next to the Martyrs, the largest category of Athonite saints. I shall present four of them, in chronological order: Athanasios the Athonite, Maximos Kafsokalyvitis, Akakios the Younger, and Joseph the Hesychast.

3. St. Athanasios the Athonite

St. Athanasios was born about 930 in Trebizond, Asia Minor, of noble, well-to-do and very devout parents. He was educated in Trebizond and Constantinople. As a student he showed unusual intelligence, thirst for learning, diligence, and exceptional self-control. Having a strong inclination towards monasticism, he became a monk at an early age at the Monastery of St. Michael Maleinos on the slopes of Mt. Kyminas, near Bursa, Asia Minor. After four years there, as a disciple of St. Michael Maleinos, he left for Athos in order to live in greater solitude. Here he led for years a very austere hermit life and attained illumination. Subsequently he established the great monastery of Lavra with money given by his close personal friend Nikephoros Phocas, first when he was a general and later when he became Emperor of Byzantium. The construction began in 963; and Athanasios organized the monastic community, writing its *Typikon* or Set of Rules that should regulate the life of the brotherhood. Lavra was organized as a coenobium — a monastic community where all the property was held in common, the monks ate together, and were governed by an abbot. Up to that time there had lived on Athos a small number of hermits, scattered and unorganized. By founding the Great Lavra, St. Athanasios became the father of coenobitic monasticism on the Holy Mountain. Its establishment was followed by that of other Athonite monasteries in the 10th and subsequent centuries, modeled after Lavra.

Many miracles are attributed to Athanasios the Athonite by his biographer, who lived in the time of the successor of the saint. In very old frescoes which survive on Athos — such as that by Panselinos in the Church of the Protaton at Karyes, and one in the Chapel of St. Anthimos in the Monastery of St. Paul — he is depicted as a rather old man with austere but serene countenance full of humility. His memory is celebrated on July 5. The kontakion which is chanted that day in his honor says:

> "Having taken upon thee the yoke of Christ, O Athanasios, and borne the cross upon thy shoulders, thou didst become a splendid imitator of His sufferings and a sharer of His glory, partaking of the unending Divine bliss."

4. *Maximos Kafsokalyvitis*

A native of Lampsacus by the Hellespont, St. Maximos Kafsokalyvitis was the son of very devout parents, who named him at Baptism Manuel. His teachers being monks, the fire of love of God was kindled in him at an early age, and he longed for a life of solitude and prayer. He was tonsured a monk at the age of seventeen by an elder who dwelt in monastic seclusion on Mount Ganos, and his name was changed to Maximos. After a time at Ganos, he went to Mount Papikion, within the boundaries of present-day Bulgaria. Here he dwelt with some other hermits who were dedicated completely to God.

Having gone to Thessaloniki to venerate St. Demetrios, the patron saint of that city, Maximos heard marvellous accounts of the Holy Mountain of Athos, and decided to visit it. His pilgrimage to Athos resulted in his becoming a life-long inhabitant there. He chose the Monastery of Lavra, and dwelt in it for a time. Later he went and lived in the wilderness, in an abrupt distant region of the Mountain belonging to Lavra. He dwelt here for many years. Then he settled at a hermitage only half an hour away from the monastery.

During his early period in the desert, he had no permanent domicile. Wishing to enjoy the greatest possible solitude, whenever anyone discovered his hut — which he built with branches and grass — he set it on fire and constructed another one elsewhere. This practice led to his being called *Kafsokalyvitis,* "he who burns huts." The wilderness where he lived subsequently became a skete named after him Kafsokalyvia. Maximos gave up this practice as a

ST. ATHANASIOS THE ATHONITE
Fresco by Manuel Panselinos. XIVth century.
Church of the Protaton, Karyes.

1

Св. Антѡ́нїй Пече́рскїй

РАБО́ТАЙТЕ
ГО́СПОДЕВИ
СО СТРА́ХОМ
Z, Й РА́ДУЙТ
ЕСА ЕМУ СZ
ТРЕ́ПЕТОМZ:
АЛЛИЛУ́Їа.
·×·

ST. ANTONY PECHERSKY

Drawing based on the Svensk-Pechersk icon painted in the
XIIIth century by St. Alypy of the Pechersk Lavra. (Courtesy Holy Transfiguration Monastery, Boston.)

2

ST. NIL SORSKY
Russian panel icon.

Ἰωάννου τοῦ Κουκουζέλη
«Ἄνωθεν οἱ Προφῆται».
Εἰς ἀρχαίαν στενογραφίαν.
ἰδιόχειρον Γρηγορίου Πρωτοψάλτου.

A composition of St. John Koukouzelis in old
Byzantine notation, as copied by Gregory Protopsaltis. (From K. A. Psachos, *The Notation
of Byzantine Music,* Athens, 1917.)

4

ST. JOHN KOUKOUZELIS
Copy of a miniature contained in Codex
178 of the Monastery of Lavra.

5

ST. SYMEON NEMANYA
Fresco, Church of Studenitza,
Yugoslavia. 1314.

6

ST. SAVA, ARCHBISHOP OF SERBIA
Detail. Fresco, Church of Milesevo,
Yugoslavia, *Ca.* 1235.

ST. NIKEPHOROS THE SOLITARY
Icon drawn by Fotis Kontoglou.

8

ST. NIPHON, PATRIARCH OF CONSTANTINOPLE
Fresco. (Courtesy Ath. Martinos, *Religious
and Ethical Encyclopedia,* Athens.).

9

ST. DIONYSIOS THE ORATOR
Icon drawn by Fotis Kontoglou.
1950.

10

ST. MAXIMOS THE GREEK
Russian panel icon.

11

ST. COSMAS AITOLOS
Panel icon.

12

ST. NICODEMOS THE HAGIORITE
Icon drawn by Fotis Kontoglou.
1958.

13

MONASTERY OF ST. PAUL

The upper part of the main church and bell tower, and part of the quadrangle.

14

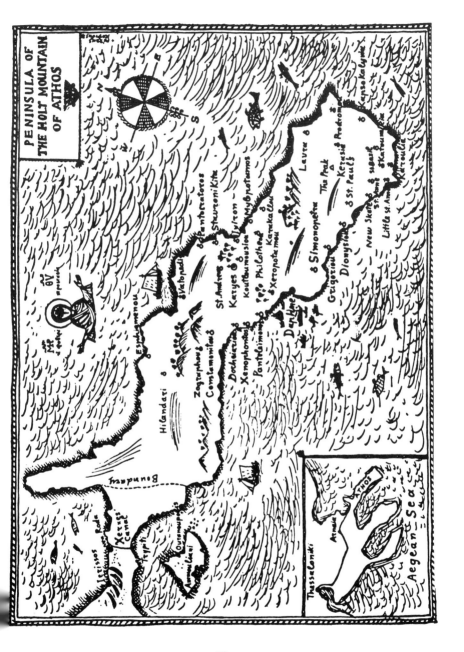

PENINSULA OF
THE HOLY MOUNTAIN
OF ATHOS

15

JOSEPH THE HESYCHAST
Photograph. 1958.

result of the strong entreaties of the famous teacher of mental prayer St. Gregory the Sinaite, who was then sojourning on Athos. Having discovered by persistent interrogating of Maximos that he was a great mystic, he urged Maximos to settle down in one place for the benefit and salvation of many.

In the *Philokalia* there is an account of a conversation Gregory had with Maximos. The latter is quoted as saying the following in connection with mental or spiritual prayer and the accompanying mystical state: "When one is pervaded by the Holy Spirit at the time of prayer, prayer ceases, because the mind is ravished by the Holy Spirit and cannot release its powers, but submits completely, and is led as the Holy Spirit wills, either to the realm of the immaterial and ineffable Divine light, or to some other amazing vision, or to a transcendent Divine converse; and the Comforter bestows His gifts upon His servant as He wills and according to one's worthiness." He is also quoted as saying: "When the mind of man is caught by that Divine light, and is illumined with Divine knowledge, his heart becomes calm and exceedingly gentle, and gushes forth the fruits of the Holy Spirit — joy, peace, longsuffering, kindness, compassion, love, humility, and so on. And the soul enjoys an inexpressible exultation. . . . This is why I have sought the wilderness and have always longed for quietness: in order to enjoy more the fruits of prayer."[5]

Maximos' biographers tell us that he was often seen surrounded by supernatural light as he stood at prayer. They also say that he possessed to a quite astonishing degree the gifts of prophecy and of reading the hidden thoughts of men; and they give many instances in which these gifts manifested themselves.

Reports of his most holy way of life, as well as of his extraordinary spiritual attainments, prompted an increasing number of persons to visit him. His hermitage became a veritable shrine. People from all walks of life, including kings and patriarchs, came to see him and ask for his counsel. Thus, in 1351 the co-rulers of the Byzantine Empire John Palaiologos and John Cantacuzenos came to him. The hermit foretold many things that were going to happen to them. Every one of his prophecies was fulfilled. Maximos prophesied, for example, that Cantacuzenos would become a monk; and four years later this emperor did indeed "exchange the royal purple for the humble black cloak of the monk."[6] He became a monk at the Monastery of Manganon at Constantinople, and his name was changed to Joasaph. As to counsel, the saint told the emperors among other things the following: "Though you are kings of the earth, you ought always to look to the Heavenly King, and keep the Law as a heavenly scepter, and be the first ones to do the Divine commandments and imitate Him as far as possible in all things. . . . Teach all your subjects faith, justice, truth, love, peace, and holiness. . . ."[7]

With respect to his austere mode of life and his virtues, Maximos Kafsokalyvitis is comparable to the great early ascetics of Egypt. Like them, he strove for the internal wisdom that is bestowed by God, and was indifferent to secular learning, in which like St. Antony the Great he was altogether untutored.

He died on January 13, around 1320, at the age of ninety-five, leaving many disciples, of whom the best known is the Ascetic Niphon. The memory of this disciple, who is credited with many miracles, is celebrated on June 14.

St. Maximos' life was written by Theophanes of Vatopedi (14th century), and has been translated into the vernacular by Nicodemos the Hagiorite. It is included in the latter's *New Eklogion*.[8]

On January 13, when he is commemorated, this kontakion is chanted in his honor:

> "We, thy servants, praise thee in hymns, O God-bearer, as a lover of sublime contemplation and as a successful practicer of inward prayer. Being initiated in divine ascents, do thou guide unto a higher life us who cry to thee: Rejoice O holy Maximos."

5. *Akakios the Younger*

Of Maximos' later emulators the most renowned is Akakios

the Younger, also known as Akakios Kafsokalyvitis, who was in his prime towards the end of the 17th century and the beginning of the 18th. He was born of devout parents in the village of Golitsa in Agrapha, and was named at Holy Baptism Anastasios. While only an infant, he lost his father. This resulted in Anastasios' remaining illiterate; for inasmuch as he was the elder son, he had to assist his mother, performing various household tasks.

At the age of twenty-three, being moved by love for the spiritual life, he went to the Monastery of Sourvia, in the vicinity of Volos. After being duly tested here, he was tonsured a monk and was renamed Akakios. Later he went to Athos, where he believed he would find superior conditions for spiritual development. He dwelt in various parts of the Holy Mountain, and finally settled at Kafsokalyvia. Here he chose a cave which had been occupied by Maximos Kafsokalyvitis and is still to be seen with Akakios' bed, consisting of a few logs.

Like Maximos, who was his chief exemplar, Akakios led a very austere life of spiritual endeavor. He kept the inner man busy with prayer and the outer man, the body, active with the handicraft of making wooden spoons. In order to subdue the passions and make unceasing prayer possible, he cultivated indifference to cold, heat, and fatigue; restricted his fare to bread, water, wild herbs and chestnuts, and partook of these only every two or three days; and slept no more than half an hour, believing that for a true monk half an hour's sleep is enough. He practiced mental prayer, particularly the form known as the Jesus Prayer.

Leading such a life, Akakios became a recipient of Divine grace and acquired, like Maximos, unusual powers. He contemplated divine visions and manifested the gifts of foreknowledge and the ability to know the inmost thoughts and dispositions of others. Also, he was often seen by his disciples and by others enveloped by supernatural light as he stood praying.

His reputation as a holy man gradually spread far and wide. Numerous persons came to him for his counsel and prayers: "bishops and priests, rulers and subjects, young and old, monks and laymen."[9] Among St. Akakios' distinguished visitors was the

Patriarch of Jerusalem Chrysanthos. The latter went to Athos as a pilgrim; and having heard of this holy man, went to see him. Chrysanthos had been educated at European higher institutions of learning, where miracles attributed to saints were dismissed as fictions, and he went to Akakios specially to determine whether there was any basis in fact for the miraculous phenomena that had been attributed to him. After staying with the saint for a time, Chrysanthos departed a great admirer of him and fully convinced that what he had heard about Akakios was true, that "the Saint saw the hidden thoughts of each man and beheld future events as if they were present."[10]

Many monks gathered around Akakios and built huts for themselves; and with their help he built dwellings where the visitors could rest. As more hermits settled in this region, Kafsokalyvia became a full-fledged skete. Its *Typikon* was first published seven years after Akakios' death. The saint fell asleep on April 12, 1750, at the age of nearly a hundred.

St. Akakios is commemorated on that day. His apolytikion says:

> "Having taken the Cross of the Lord upon thy
> shoulders, thou didst follow after him even till
> the end of thy sojourn in the world, and thou
> didst disdain the enjoyment of earthly things,
> for thy soul was pierced with His love from thy
> youth on, O wise one, and thou didst struggle
> well in the ascetical life, O God-bearing Akakios.
> Do thou protect us by thine intercessions with
> God."

His akoluthia and an excellent account of his life have been written by his disciple Priestmonk Jonas Kafsokalyvitis. These are preserved in manuscript form in the library of Kafsokalyvia. The life has been published in the *New Martyrologium* and in collections of lives of saints. Although Akakios did not suffer martyrdom, his life is included at the end of the *New Martyrologium* because he was a "trainer of martyrs." Three of his disciples were put to death by the Turks for boldly professing the Christian faith. They were St. Romanos of Karpenisi, Greece, St. Nicodemos of Elbasan, Albania, and St. Pachomios of Russia. Romanos suffered martyrdom on January 15, 1694, at Constantinople; Nicodemos, on July 11, 1722, at Belgrade; and Pachomios, on May 7, 1730, at Ushak, Asia Minor.

In his book *History of Asceticism: Athonites,*[11] Evlogios Kourilas of the Monastery of Lavra deals at length with Akakios the Younger, as well as with his great predecessor Maximos Kafso-kalyvitis and the Skete of Kafsokalyvia.

6. *Joseph the Hesychast*

The last Ascetic I shall discuss, Joseph the Hesychast, is of special significance as a very influential reviver of the systematic practice of mental prayer. I devoted a number of pages to him in *Anchored in God,* which was published in July, 1959, only a month before his death. My account was based on a meeting I had with him in the spring of the previous year at the New Skete, a depend-ency of the Monastery of St. Paul. I noted then that Father Joseph "impressed me as being a genuine mystic, a true saint." I used the term saint to characterize him, because I was convinced that he met the Orthodox criteria of sainthood, which I have stated earlier. This term was applied to him a few months later by Soterios Schoinas, editor and publisher of the periodical *Hagi-orite Library,* in his obituary which appeared in that publication. Expressing his own conviction and that of many others, both on Athos and elsewhere in Greece, Schoinas remarked: "The death of Joseph is regarded as that of a saint."[12]

In the account which follows I shall not repeat what I have written in *Anchored in God,* but will draw my material from the article of Schoinas just mentioned, and from a 75-page manuscript entitled *The Life of Our Evermemorable Father Joseph the Hesy-chast,*[13] written in 1962 by his disciple Joseph, a monk at the New Skete.

Joseph's name before he became a monk was Frangiskos, "Francis." He was born around the year 1894 in Paros, one of the Cyclades Islands. After attending school for about two years, he was sent by his destitute parents to Piraeus in order to work and support himself, and later to help his younger brothers and sisters. After working for a time at a grocery store as an errand boy, he went to Athens and became a merchant. Thanks to his intelligence and thrift, Frangiskos' venture as a merchant was successful. He was not only able to send considerable financial aid home, but could seriously hope some day to be a wealthy man.

But later his interests began to turn away from money-making. One day a kindly neighbor gave him a copy of Agapios the Cretan's *Kalokairine* to read during his leisure hours. The lives of the saints narrated in this book aroused his interest in religion, until then dormant. He began wondering about the truthfulness of these amazing biographies. In order to find out, he started visiting popular shrines, such as the Monastery of St. Gerasimos in Cephalonia and the Church of the Theotokos in Tinos, where miraculous events were said to occur every year. These pilgrimages had the effect of dispelling the doubts which he had about the possibility of the miracles attributed to the saints in *Kalokairine*. For at these holy places he both heard of similar phenomena from persons he met, and witnessed some himself. Afterwards, Frangiskos met a monk from the Holy Mountain who spoke to him about the Mountain and how the monks there lived. This made him eager to visit Athos at his first opportunity.

His desire to go there was fulfilled at the age of twenty-three, after he had served in the navy for the required period of time. Once there, he decided to stay. Having a strong aspiration to cultivate the interior life, he searched for a suitable place of stillness and a good spiritual guide. This quest led him to some of the remotest hermitages. He dwelt in succession at Katounakia, just above the awesome Karoulia, at Vigla, near the Rumanian Skete of Prodromou, again at Katounakia, at St. Basil, on the southwestern slope of Mount Carmel, at the Small Skete of St. Anne, and finally, from 1951 to the time of his repose, at the New Skete. His best spiritual guide was an old hermit named Ephraim. This very pious and wise monk was his elder for years at Katounakia and then at St. Basil's.

Joseph led an exceedingly austere life of spiritual endeavor, observing the greatest strictness in all things. Above all he devoted himself to mental prayer, both during the fixed periods set aside for it during the day and the night, and while he practiced his handicraft of making small wooden crosses. He mastered the arts of inner attention and spiritual prayer, and taught them successfully to a growing number of followers. This interior life, he stressed, constitutes the essence of true monasticism, lifting the monk to the higher Christian virtues and making him a partaker of Divine grace.

Through this way of life, spiritual love steadily increased in him, purifying completely the soul and rendering it an abode of the Spirit. He experienced such love for and from God, that he wept copiously, overwhelmed by humility and feelings of gratitude for God's boundless love for His creatures. And he felt so much love for his fellow men, that were it possible, he would have taken upon himself the sufferings of all men and died for them in order to lift them to the blessedness of God. Also, Joseph became a remarkable seer and mystic, who rose to states of consciousness similar to those experienced by the great hesychasts of the past.

By way of example, I shall cite from the manuscript *Father Joseph the Hesychast* the following statement made by this holy elder:

"There comes a time, as a person is practicing mental prayer with all his thoughts gathered together, invoking the sweet name of our Lord Jesus, when suddenly the mind is illumined or rather is caught by a boundless immaterial light, white as snow, and a subtle fragrance pervades all his members; and he transcends himself, stands in another creation transfigured. He no longer prays then, nor thinks, but only contemplates and marvels at the Divine magnificence."

Joseph fell asleep on August 15, 1959, by the old calendar, the day of the Dormition of the Holy Virgin Mary whom he greatly revered, and the day of the repose of Cephalonia's patron saint

Gerasimos, whose life was a major source of inspiration for him from the time he visited the convent of this saint.

Since his departure, Father Joseph's reputation as a teacher of mental prayer, spiritual guide and saint has been growing. In less than ten years his followers at the New Skete increased from eight to forty. Being too many for the existing dwellings, twenty of them under Hieromonk Ephraim have moved to an abandoned Russian kelli at Provata, a dependency of Lavra, and twelve others headed by Hieromonk Haralambos have gone to a deserted kelli near Karyes.

EPILOGUE

I shall conclude my discussion on the scholars, missionaries, and saints of Mount Athos by saying a few more words about the way of life that has been followed by them and in general by the monks of Athos through the centuries. This way involves two kinds of methods or practices, two kinds of "work" (*ergasia*), as the Greek Fathers call them: physical and mental or spiritual. Among the physical practices are fasting, continence, vigils, kneelings or prostrations, standing motionless at prayer, reading, chanting, manual work. These are viewed as important instruments for the spiritual practices. Spiritual "work" includes confession, concentration, meditation, inner attention, love, private prayer, and corporate prayer — worship in church.

The reason for employing physical as well as spiritual methods is the Orthodox belief that man is made up of body and soul, and that the state of the one affects the state of the other. Right physical practices are viewed as having good effects on the soul or spirit, and right spiritual practices as producing good effects on the body. This point is brought out beautifully by the following passage from the *Ladder* of St. John Climacos, one of the favorite books on Mount Athos: "It is amazing to see the incorporeal mind being defiled and darkened by the body, and again the immaterial mind being purified and refined through clay." [15]

Both physical and spiritual practices have as their ultimate end the transformation of the soul, the restoration of the divine image in man to likeness to God, and thereby the attainment of *theosis*, participation in God's perfection and blessedness, salvation.[2]

The desire to help their Christian brethren far and wide attain this goal has led many qualified monks to engage in writing, publishing, and missionary activities. It has also inspired them and countless

73

other monks to offer valuable counsel and heart-felt prayers for their fellow monks as well as for pilgrims.

PART TWO

MUSIC, MUSICIANS, AND HYMNOGRAPHERS

CHAPTER I

MUSIC

In one of his letters, addressed to his friend Gregory of Nazianzus, in which he endeavors to induce Gregory to join him in his monastic life, Basil the Great says: "What is more blessed than to imitate on earth the anthems of angels' choirs; to hasten to prayer at the very break of day, and to worship the Creator with hymns and songs; then, when the sun shines brightly and we turn to our tasks, prayer attending us wherever we go, to season our labors with sacred song as food with salt? For the state of the soul in which there is joy and no sorrow is a boon bestowed by the consolation of hymns." [1] And in his *Longer Rules* for the monastic life, Basil says: "For prayer and psalmody, as for many other things, every time is suitable; so that we praise God with psalms and hymns and spiritual songs, while we move our hands in work, chanting with our tongue if this is possible and conducive to the edification of the faith, but if not, then in the heart." [2] The life despicted by this saint, in which sacred music occupies such an important place, has been adopted by Athonite monasticism since its origin more than a thousand years ago. The pattern set and the rules formulated by St. Basil in the 4th century, St. Theodore the Studite in the 9th, and St. Athanasios the Athonite in the 10th, still regulate the life of the monasteries of Athos, particularly of the coenobitic ones, which represent a stricter form of monasticism.

Theodore the Studite is known as one of the outstanding hymnographers of the Orthodox Church. At the Monastery of Studium (at Constantinople), of which Theodore was abbot, he, his brother Joseph and other monks practiced the art of composing church hymns and songs. Besides writing such poetry, Theodore taught the monks the art of chanting.[3] At the Studium, "the singing of psalms did not go on only in the church; . . . the brethren

77

were instructed to sing certain psalms while engaged in their several occupations." [4] Athanasios the Athonite, who in 963 founded the first monastery of the Holy Mountain, that of Lavra, similarly assigned great importance to music in the monastic life. Thus, in his biography we read that he ordained that the monks should sing hymns to the Lord during the day and night services; and that no one should speak or be inattentive during the chanting. Also, he placed at the head of each of the two choirs a brother, whom he called the *epistemonarches,* whose duty was to concern himself with the proper appearance of the chanters and with the good state of their souls. Evidently, St. Athanasios regarded the former as necessary for impressing on the congregation the importance of sacred music, and the latter as necessary for its proper execution.

The life of the monks of Athos is probably the most musical one led by a community anywhere on earth. Typically, about six hours a day are devoted to church services that consist almost entirely of chanting. These services are the *orthros* or matins, the Divine Liturgy, the vespers, and the *apodeipnon* or compline. On an average of once a week, there is a rather long service called *agrypnia,* "vigil," which commences in the evening before a major holy day and continues for twelve or more hours. This means that there is almost continuous chanting for twelve hours or longer about fifty times a year.

From the very beginning down to the present eighteen of Athos' twenty monasteries and their dependencies have used Byzantine music. Of these, seventeen are Greek and one is Bulgarian. The other two, the Russian and the Serbian, also employed Byzantine music from the time they were founded, many centuries ago, until recent times. The Russians introduced Russian music in the last century; the Serbs, Serbian music in the nineteen-thirties. Russian and Serbian music is basically Western. The other important group of non-Greek monks, the Rumanians, have never abandoned Byzantine music. They use this music in their two monastery-like sketes and their smaller monastic establishments.

1. *Purely Vocal Music*

The music used on Athos has always• been purely vocal, no

instruments whatsoever being used either for its execution or accompaniment. In this respect Athonite monasticism has been absolutely faithful to the practice and teaching of the Fathers of the Orthodox Church, who established that only vocal music be used in the churches, and severely forbade instrumental music as being secular and in general as evoking pleasure without spiritual value. Musical instruments have been viewed by the Fathers as among the things of the "broad" as opposed to the "narrow way" spoken of by Jesus, being associated with drinking, dancing, laughter, shouts, luxury and the like. The following statement of Nicodemos the Hagiorite, in the Introduction of his *Heortodromion,* illustrates this position:

"Hymns to God were executed by the Jews with instruments. But since God rejected their instruments — as He said through Amos: 'Remove from me the sound of thy songs, and I will not hear the music of thine instruments' [5] — we Christians execute our hymns through the voice alone." [6]

On the Holy Mountain the playing of musical instruments of any sort is forbidden not only in the churches, but everywhere else. Playing musical instruments or listening to them is considered quite alien to the monastic vocation. Even the possession of a musical instrument is forbidden.

2. *Homophony*

Byzantine music is homophonic. This means that there is only one part, so that even when many chanters participate in the psalmody they all chant together, as though their voices were coming out of one mouth. On the Mountain the music is homophonic not only in the eighteen monasteries and their dependencies which use Byzantine chant, but also in the Serbian monastery. Only the chanting of the Russians is polyphonic — they use four-part harmony.

Polyphonic chanting is an innovation that was introduced into Russian churches from the West in the 18th century, when the Russian church underwent Westernization in its iconography and theology as well as its music. Later, Russians coming to the Holy Mountain and embracing the monastic life introduced polyphony to the Monastery of Panteleimonos, known as the Russian Monastery, and to the Russian sketes and *kellia.*

3. *Antiphony*

Antiphony is another characteristic of Byzantine music also preserved on Athos. The *katholika* or main churches are all designed for two choirs, one on the north and one on the south side of the nave. There is an outward projection of the edifice here, forming an apse which internally provides a spacious semicircular area known as *choros*, "choir." Here the chanters take their places in stalls that line the semicircular wall. The middle stall is occupied by the leading chanter. In front of him is an octagonal *analogion* or book stand with a revolving top on which the liturgical books are placed. Windows in the apse provide ample lighting for the chanters in the daytime, while a suspended oil lamp above the *analogion* provides light for them during the night services. (Electrical lighting is not used on Athos.)

When a particular monastery or skete is celebrating the memory of the sacred personage or event to which its main church is dedicated, monks from other parts of the Mountain as well as laymen come to worship, so that not only the nave but also the narthexes are filled. The chanters then stand at the eastern side of the *choros*, facing westward, towards the congregation, so that their voices may carry farther and be heard distinctly by all. Gifted, well-trained chanters from other monasteries or sketes come and join in the chanting. The music on such occasions is truly magnificent and very moving, invoking deep religious awe and joy, the "gladdening sorrow" of which St. John Climacos speaks in his *Ladder of Divine Ascent.*

As a rule, here as elsewhere in Greece, the better, more experienced chanters occupy the choir on the right (south) side of the church. The two choirs alternate: first the right choir sings then the left, then the right again, and so on throughout the service. This practice is called antiphony. In monastic establishments which employ Byzantine or Serbian chant, antiphony can be employed even when there are only two chanters, there being only one part to be executed by each choir using such music.

4. *Canonarchema*

Another feature of the music of Athos is the *canonarchema,* "the leading of the canon" or chant. One of the younger monks, the prompter (*kanonarches*), goes from one of the choirs to the other, and reads in an intoned loud voice what the chanter or choir is about to psalmodize. He reads one phrase of a troparion, and the chanter psalmodizes that; then he reads the next one, and so on, until the entire troparion has been chanted. Thereupon, he walks over to the other choir and begins reading the next troparion.

The *canonarchema* is done on the basic tone of the mode in which the melody is being chanted, and thus takes the place of the *ison* or holding of the basic tone by one or more chanters. It is employed in the case of the troparia of the Beatitudes (*Makarismoi*) of the Liturgy and in many parts of the vespers and the orthros.

This practice has puzzled some persons who have visited Athos. Thus, R.M. Dawkins remarks in his book *The Monks of Athos*: "By an extraordinary archaism it is supposed in many parts of the service that the singers cannot read, and they are assisted by a prompter, who in a loud voice goes through each verse always about a phrase ahead of the singer, so that the two are singing at the same time, but different words, a system which to anyone who does not know the service by heart is as confusing as anything well could be." [7] Dawkins' theory that the canonarchema owes its origin to the scarcity of books in the past and to illiteracy is plausible; but other explanations of it can be given. That it sometimes causes confusion is undoubtedy true — true when it is not properly used. When rightly employed, it enables the congregation to hear clearly all the words and phrases of the hymns, and gives the chanter momentary periods of rest. Right use of the canonarchema consists in the prompter reading clearly and at an unhurried tempo, and in the chanter giving the prompter time to finish the verse or phrase before he begins to sing it. [8]

The canonarchema adds useful variety to the service, helping to keep the congregation alert, and provides valuable musical training for younger monks, being their first step in becoming chanters. But its chief value lies in helping the congregation hear distinctly all the words and phrases of hymns that are chanted slowly, with frequent repetition of vowels.

5. *Execution*

The importance of the proper execution of hymns has been stressed by Hagiorite authors. They emphasize the need of psalmodizing attentively, not letting the mind wander from the meaning of what is being chanted. Attention is necessary if the hymn is to be properly executed, and if benefit is to be derived from it as a form of prayer by him who sings it and by those who listen. Thus, Theoleptos of Philadelphia advises: "Having gathered together in the Lord with your brethren, just as you adopt the proper attitude with your body, and with your tongue psalmodize to the Lord, so keep your mind attentive to the words and to God, realizing with Whom it is conversing." [9] And Callistos and Ignatios Xanthopoulos say: "Chant very attentively and with understanding." [10]

The Athonites also emphasize the need of psalmodizing with devoutness, without ostentation or unduly loud voice. Thus, the same Theoleptos counsels: "Psalmodize with an altogether unforced voice." [11] And in the biography of St. Simon, founder of the Monastery of Simonopetra (14th century), we read that towards the end of his life he gave the following directions to the monks: "At the church services chant with solemnity and devoutness, and not with disorderly vociferations." [12] Similarly, Nicodemos the Hagiorite says: "The psalmody which takes place in the church is an entreaty to God . . . . Now he who makes an entreaty and prays must be in a state of humility and contrition; whereas an unduly loud voice manifests audacity and irreverence." [13] Again, he remarks: "Cantors should psalmodize in a reverent and orderly manner, with fear of God, piety and contrition." [14]

Nicodemos has written against the excessively slow execution of some compositions, such as the *Communion Hymn,* where there is a prolonged repetition of the same syllable, and against the great prolongation of other hymns by "Te-re-rems," known as *kratemata,* "holdings-back." The chanting thereby becomes tedious to the congregation and the meaning of the hymns is lost. He advises that such hymns be chanted at a faster tempo and the time thus saved be used for reading some edifying passages. [15]

Today, chanting on the Holy Mountain generally shows due regard for these requirements for the proper execution of the music.

6. *Function of Chanting*

Chanting has been recognized on Athos as one of the major kinds of "work" or activity that should be performed by a monk. It is a form of prayer in which both the soul and the body participate. Its psycho-physical character distinguishes chanting from purely psychical or mental prayer. The latter is the highest form of prayer and of activity in general, according to Orthodox teaching. Such prayer is carried on solely by the rational faculty and the emotional center or "heart." Mental prayer is superior to psalmodizing, but much more difficult to practice, because it requires great concentration, the suppression of the senses, of imagination, and of discursive thought. Hence the prolonged practice of this form of prayer is reserved for those who are advanced in the spiritual life, and have withdrawn from the monastery to a hermitage, to a place of greatest quietness. These are the hesychasts, the mystics. In their case mental prayer takes the place of the matins and the compline, which occupy the monks in the monasteries about three hours daily; and thus the amount of psalmodizing done by hesychasts is considerably reduced.

The chief value of psalmodizing is as a form of prayer. Through it, say the Hagiorite Fathers, one becomes a recipient of Divine grace, which purifies the soul of bad thoughts and emotions, and illuminates it. Thus, Nicodemos remarks: "Where there are spiritual melodies there comes the grace of the Spirit, sanctifying the mouth and the soul." [16]

Because psalmody is an effective means of opposing and overcoming negative inner elements, it is spoken of as a "weapon" by Callistos and Ignatios Xanthopoulos and by other Fathers who dwelt on the Holy Mountain.

Among the other important values of chanting cited by Hagiorites are an augmented consciousness and understanding of the meanings contained in hymns, and a consequent more Christian way of life. Theoleptos observes in this connection: "If you know

what you are chanting, you acquire consciousness of what you know;
from this consciousness you acquire understanding; and from understanding springs putting into practice what you have become
conscious of."[17]

MUSICIANS AND HYMNOGRAPHERS

Numerous distinguished cantors, hymnographers, music theorists and teachers have appeared on the Holy Mountain through the centuries. In his authoritative book *Athos,* which was published in 1885 at Constantinople, Manuel Gedeon says: "There have appeared on Athos more cantors and musicians than anywhere else in the Orthodox East. The musical manuscripts at Athos disclose to us a great number of musicians; and of each musician there survive one or more compositions." [1]

1. *St. John Koukouzelis*

The most famous cantor, hymnographer and music theorist of the Holy Mountain is John Koukouzelis (or Cucuzelis), who lived in the 12th century. He has been characterized as the second fount of music after John Damascene. Having become very proficient in sacred music at Constantinople, and possessing a voice of quite extraordinary beauty, Koukouzelis was appointed leader of the imperial chanters. But as he yearned for the quiet, undistracted life of prayer led by monks, he gave up his brilliant musical career at the capital of Byzantium and went to Athos, where he became a monk at the Monastery of Lavra. Despite his efforts to live here incognito, his identity was discovered, and he was made *Protopsaltis* or First Cantor of the monastery.

While a monk at Lavra, he composed a book on the art of music and one containing church hymns with musical notation. Also, he melodized Cherubic Hymns in the eight Modes of Byzantine music, a Communion Hymn, and numerous other liturgical poems, including calophonic hirmi, which are hymns of a very artistic nature.

St. John is of special significance in the history of Byzantine music, because he introduced changes in the musical notation that had been developed by John Damascene, and instilled new life into Byzantine chant.[2]

His memory is celebrated on October 1. The kontakion which is sung in his honor says:

> "Having been wounded by Christ, thou, of honored name, didst run with zeal the course of spiritual endeavor; and having devoted thy time to hymns, spiritual songs and odes, thou hast pleased God. And now thou intercedest in heaven for us all."

2. St. Gregory the Domestikos

Among the pupils of John Koukouzelis was Gregory the Domestikos (leading chanter), also called, after his master, Gregory *Koukouzelis*. Like John, whom he succeeded as First Cantor of the Monastery of Lavra, Gregory became a famous musician.

In his book on Athos, Gedeon remarks about John and Gregory Koukouzelis: "The renowned musician (John) Koukouzelis has been classified among the saints of our Church, and is honored on October 1st together with another musician of the Monastery of Lavra, Gregory the Domestikos. He chanted in the right choir of Lavra, as did Gregory. Both were admired for their art and sweetness of voice. Of both it is said that the Theotokos appeared to them as they chanted in their stalls and presented them with gold coins." [3] And G. I. Papadopoulos, the most important Greek historian of Byzantine music and hymnography, notes about Gregory that "he was a most skillful musician, who at the vigil services chanted continuously with piety and contrition, never sitting down in the church." [4]

3. Theoleptos of Philadelphia

After Sts. John and Gregory, during the reign of Andronikos Palaiologos (1282-1328), remarkable contributions were made by Theoleptos of Philadelphia and Theodoulos Thekaras. Theoleptos composed various contrite hymns, among them four canons: one on the Final Judgment, one to Jesus Christ, and two to the Theotokos.[5]

4. Theodoulos Thekaras

Theodoulos Thekaras composed hymns and authored two "methods" or handbooks on the art of chanting which are preserved in one of the manuscripts of the Monastery of Leimonos in Lesvos. He is regarded as the author of *Thekaras,* a book that contains prayers and numerous liturgical hymns, most of them addressed to the Holy Trinity and to the Theotokos. *Thekaras* first appeared in print in 1643 at Venice, edited by Agapios Landos, and has been reprinted many times since then. Theodoulos has also been regarded as the author of some canons in the eight Modes in honor of the Theotokos, chanted in monasteries daily after the vespers.[6]

5. *St. Philotheos the Patriarch*

The next important figure is Philotheos, who flourished in the early part of the 14th century, served as abbot of Lavra and later became Patriarch of Constantinople. He composed many canons, including a canon of entreaty to our Lord and canons to St. Nicholas and to St. John Chrysostom. He also composed akoluthias, among them one commemorating the Fathers of the Fourth Ecumenical Synod and one in honor of St. Gregory Palamas, and various troparia to the Theotokos.[7]

6. *Synesios the Hagiorite*

Synesios the Hagiorite, who was a native of Mytilene and lived before the fall of Constantinople, composed Cherubic, Communion and other hymns.[8]

7. *Gerasimos Halkiopoulos*

A Domestikos at Athos, Gerasimos Halkiopoulos (fl. middle of the 15th century), distinguished himself as a cantor and melodist. He melodized eight Cherubic hymns and various other compositions.[9]

8. *Cosmas of Iviron*

The best known Athonite musician of the subsequent period prior to the 18th century is Cosmas of Iviron. He was a Domestikos of that monastery and flourished towards the end of the 17th century. An excellent musician, Cosmas melodized many hymns, among them the *Katabasiai* of the Annunciation.[10]

9. *Damianos of Vatopedi*

According to data contained in histories of Byzantine music, the 18th century was the most remarkable period of Mount Athos in the field of music. During that century it produced the following outstanding hymnographers and musicians: Damianos of Vatopedi, Panayotis Halatzoglous, Peter Glykis, Nicodemos the Hagiorite, Neophytos Kafsokalyvitis, Kaisarios Dapontes, and Christophoros Artinos.

Damianos of Vatopdi (fl. 1740) was an excellent cantor and teacher of the art of chanting at Vatopedi, and also a melodist, having set to melody many hymns, including *kratemata* and *calophonic hirmi*. His musical compositions are distinguished for their clarity and strict adherence to the style of Byzantine ecclesiastical music. He trained many in this music, among them two of the most outstanding musicians of that period: Halatzoglous and Glykis.[11]

10. *Panayotis Halatzoglous*

Halatzoglous became First Cantor of the church of the Patriarchate at Constantinople, and served in that capacity from 1728 to 1748, the year of his death. Also, he melodized many hymns and wrote a small manual on Byzantine music and a study entitled *Comparison of Arabo-persian Music with Our Own Ecclesiastical,*[12] which was published in 1728 in the periodical of the Ecclesiastical Musical Society of Constantinople. Like his master, Halatzoglous trained many in the theory and practice of Byzantine music. Some of them became widely known — for example, John of Trebizond, who succeeded him as First Cantor of the church of the Patriarchate at Constantinople, Daniel of Tyrnavos, who chanted with John, and Cyril, Archbishop of Tinos.[13]

11. *Peter Glykis (Bereketis)*

Trained by both Damianos and Halatzoglous, Peter Glykis, also known as Bereketis (fl. 1768), became one of the most remarkable melodists and musicians of the Greek Church after the fall of Constantinople. He melodized numerous liturgical hymns, including hirmi, doxologies, Communion and Cherubic hymns. Having distinguished himself above all others in the melodizing of calophonic hirmi, he has been called the father of such hirmi. He served for many years as First Cantor of the Church of St. Constantine at Constantinople.

Bereketis and Halatzoglous were not monks. They were lay-men, natives of Constantinople, who went to the Holy Mountain for the purpose of studying Byzantine music and becoming proficient in chanting in the true Byzantine style.[14]

12. *St. Nicodemos the Hagiorite*

Nicodemos embellished the hymns and encomia of the *Epita-phios* and of Easter, and corrected many canons, especially those of the *Theotokarion* — a book containing canons in honor of the Theotokos in all eight modes of Byzantine music, chanted by monks daily after the *apodeipnon*. Also, he composed numerous canons and akoluthias, including an akoluthia commemorating all the saints of Athos.[15] He is a very important hymnographer of the Greek Church.

It should be noted that Nicodemos as well as the other modern Greek hymnographers of Athos wrote in the language and style of the great hymnographers of Byzantium.

13. *Other Hymnographers and Musicians*

Regarding the other 18th century hymnographers and musicians I have mentioned, the following facts are particularly worth noting. Neophytos Kafsokalyvitis wrote a book on music, and the akoluthia of Sts. Barnabas, Christopher and Sophronios of Mount Melas. [16] Dapontes, of the Monastery of Xeropotamou, composed various hymns, including canons and salutations.[17] Christophoros Artinos (b. 1730), who dwelt first in the New Skete and then at Iviron's Skete of Prodromou, wrote various melodic hymns.[18]

In the 19th century, two Hagiorite monks gained considerable repute as cantors: Nectarios Vlachos and Theotokis of Vatopedi. Nectarios (fl. second half of the century), a native of Wallachia, was for half a century First Cantor of the Rumanian Skete of Pro-dromou, a dependency of Lavra, and also led the chanting at festal vigils of the monasteries of the Holy Mountain. He melodized various hymns.[19] Theotokis (d. 1884), a native of Mytilene, became First Cantor of the Monastery of Vatopedi. He trained many in

Byzantine chant. Both Nectarios and Theotokis possessed voices of extraordinary beauty.[20]

In recent years, Father Gerasimos Mikragiannanitis, of the Small Skete of Saint Anne, has acquired eminence as a hymnographer, having authored a book of apolytikia, kontakia and megalynaria intended for the use of cantors and choirs on Sundays, feasts and other days throughout the year,[21] and also composed numerous akoluthias, supplicatory canons, and troparia.[22] Of special interest among his akoluthias are those in honor of modern saints, such as Dionysios the Orator, Nicodemos the Hagiorite, Arsenios the Younger, and Nectarios.

14. *Concluding Remarks*

Not only has Byzantine music been cultivated and preserved on Athos down to the present, as a living art, but it has been preserved in a purer form than at other centers of Orthodoxy. Writing in 1885, Gedeon called attention to the fact that in the early part of the 18th century the Byzantine style of chanting had fallen into disuse and was ignored at the very city which had been the capital of the Byzantine empire: Constantinople. It was for this reason, he remarks, that Halatzoglous left Constantinople and went to Athos.[23] Bereketis went to the Holy Mountain for the same reason. Both went there with a view to being trained in the authentic Byzantine style and then returning to Constantinople to serve as cantors in the Greek churches and to instruct others in this sacred music.

Thus, besides preserving Byzantine music for itself, Mount Athos also enabled the Orthodox to retain this precious art in other places, where it was in danger of being lost forever. If Byzantine music continues today to be sung in the churches throughout Greece, as well as in Bulgaria and elsewhere, this is to a large extent due to the monks of the Holy Mountain of Athos.

Byzantine hymnography, too, has been cultivated and preserved on Athos without interruption down to this day. Countless liturgical hymnographic works of various types, sublime in content and outstanding in literary merit, have been composed here through the centuries, evincing that the Holy Mountain has been the greatest center of Greek Orthodox hymnography during the last millenium.

PART THREE

RECENT VISIT TO ATHOS

ON THE WAY

Early in August of 1965 I commenced my fourth pilgrimage on the Holy Mountain, just seven years after my third visit. It was most rewarding, as were my previous visits, affording quite unusual opportunities for inner stillness, worship, and conversation with holy men.

The starting point of my journey to Athos was the island of Mytilene, where I had gone for the summer and fall. I boarded an old 2,000 ton steamer, mainly a freight vessel, named *Panayotis,* which plied between Rhodes and Thessaloniki stopping at the islands of Samos, Chios, Mytilene and Limnos. The *Panayotis* left the port of Mytilene at 7:30 in the evening and arrived at 4 in the morning at Limnos' port of Castro, "the Fortress," on the west side of the island. This picturesque little town is named after the fortress on the top of the nearby hill. The ship stayed here for more than an hour, during which time some passengers were taken ashore in small boats and others were brought to the steamer.

As the vessel resumed its northwestward course, dawn arrived, and an hour and a half after our departure from Limnos we began to see Athos rising magnificently above the serene waters of the Aegean. The course which the ship follows is far from Athos, and hence only the silhousette of the Mountain could be seen. But even this was a quite remarkable, unforgettable sight.

We passed closer to the middle prong of the Halkidiki Peninsula, named Sithonia or Longos, and rather close to the western prong, Cassandra. The terrain of Sithonia and Cassandra is hilly, not mountainous like Athos. Cassandra abounds in vegetation, mostly trees, such as firs, pines and olives.

The *Panayotis* arrived at Thessaloniki in the afternoon and docked in the commercial harbor. Having a few hours at my disposal before sunset, I visited some of the city's famous Byzantine churches: St. Demetrios, Acheiropoietos, and Panaghia ton Halkeon. I had visited these sacred edifices many times before; their enchanting mystical beauty is for me an inexhaustible source of inspiration.

I left for the Holy Mountain early the next day, taking a bus from the terminal at Odos Platonos, "Plato Street," off Egnatia Street in the heart of Thessaloniki. The bus left at 6:30 and arrived at Ouranoupolis, or Prosphori, near the border of the Mountain, in less than five hours. It followed the same route as in my earlier visits to the Mountain, except that then it did not go as far as Ouranoupolis, but stopped at the town of Ierissos, or the nearby village of New Roda, more than thirty kilometers from Ouranoupolis. One had to stay there overnight and then take in the morning a bus that went to the other side of the neck of the Athos peninsula, to a spot with a wooden pier known as Trypiti. From Trypiti one took a motorboat which stopped at Ouranoupolis and then headed for Daphne, the main port of Athos. Now it is not necessary to stay overnight at Ierissos — one can leave Thessaloniki in the morning and be at Athos in the afternoon.

The road to Ouranoupolis was constructed by the Greek government in 1963 — when the celebration of the one thousand years of Athonite monasticism took place — ostensibly to enable the late King Paul to drive there in his own car. Actually, this justification was only a pretext used by the government to take one more step for attracting more tourists from abroad to Greece, and for turning the Holy Mountain from a secluded place dedicated to spiritual values to an easily accessible "archeological area" serving economic ends. That the passage of the king was used only as a pretext is testified by the fact that the king did not drive to Ouranoupolis, but went to Athos by sea, disembarking from a naval vessel at the Monastery of Lavra.

At Ouranoupolis, which is a small village built near the shore, there is a Byzantine tower that was converted long ago by an Englishman named Sydney Loch into a home. Since the motor launch that takes tourists, pilgrims, and returning monks to Daphne was scheduled to leave nearly two hours after the arrival of the bus, I had ample time not only to eat at one of the recently built restaurants, but also to go to the tower. I found Mrs. Loch there, and after I explained to her who I was, she graciously invited me into the living room.

I had hoped to see her husband, who had authored the book *Athos: The Holy Mountain,* which was published in London in 1957. But I learned that he had died. Mrs. Loch told me that she was a native of Australia, came here with her husband in 1928, and settled in this tower, making it their permanent home.

The name of Father Nikon, a well-known Russian hermit, came up; and she informed me that he was a friend of theirs and died in 1964. Some months prior to his death Father Nikon broke one of his arms, but refused to go to a hospital or a physician, despite the entreaties of the Lochs. However, he did not die as a result of this, Mrs. Loch remarked, but of general debility. He was ninety-two years old. I had the good fortune of meeting this holy priest-monk twice, first at Daphne in 1952 and then at his hermitage at Karoulia in 1958.[1]

MONASTERY OF XEROPOTAMOU

The motor launch that sails daily from Trypiti to the port of Daphne picked up at 12:45 those who were waiting for it at Ouranoupolis. It arrived at Daphne in two and a half hours, after stopping briefly at the piers of the monasteries of Zographou, Docheiariou, Xenophontos, and Panteleimonos.

Upon landing at Daphne, I proceeded to the Monastery of Xeropotamou, with the intention of staying there for the night and going the next day to the village of Karyes, the capital of the Holy Mountain. Xeropotamou is on a small plateau above Daphne, about three quarters of an hour away by foot. At the entrance of the monastery I was greeted by the monk Chrysanthos, who came to the Mountain at the age of twenty-five and has been at Xeropotamou for over forty years. He led me to the guesthouse, where the guestmaster, Father Porphyry, showed me to a room where I was to rest and sleep. Later Porphyry came and invited me to the dining room of the guesthouse for supper.

This monk was then fifty-five years old, but looked much younger. He served the guests assisted by a lay cook from Ouranoupolis. The meal consisted of boiled beans with olive oil, tomato salad, potatoes, bread and wine. The tomatoes had been produced in the nearby garden without the use of chemical fertilizers, and were delicious.

"We avoid the use of chemical fertilizers," Father Porphyry remarked, "because vegetables that grow in soil where these are used not only lack the taste of naturally grown vegetables, but also are one of the major causes of the diseases that plague people today."

The *orthros* or matins began at 3:30 in the morning, or at 8 o'clock by the Byzantine system that is used by this and nearly all the other Athonite monasteries.[1] The time according to the old system is shown by the clock on a tower that bears the date 1779. I was awakened for the orthros by the rhythmic sounds of the wooden gong known as the *semantron*. The Divine Liturgy followed the orthros at 5:30. The orthros was held in the main part of the *katholikon* or principal church, at the center of the courtyard, while the Liturgy was celebrated in the side chapel of Saints Constantine and Helen.

As is customary on Athos, after the church services the priest presented the sacred relics of the monastery to the pilgrims for veneration. Among these is a fragment of the True Cross, the largest fragment in existence on Mount Athos.

I asked Father Chrysanthos, Porphyry and others about the present state of Xeropotamou. The number of monks, I learned, had not changed since my previous visit. There were thirty monks. One of the most pious brothers of the monastery whom I met in 1958, Gregory of Larissa, the baker, left in 1963 and went to the Monastery of St. Paul, apparently because he developed a preference for the stricter coenobitic system of St. Paul's to the idiorrhythmic system of Xeropotamou. His place was soon taken by another monk.

A further noteworthy fact I learned is that the construction work which commenced long ago to restore about a third of the monastery that had been destroyed by fire in 1951 had been halted. The destroyed edifices, consisting of cells, have been rebuilt, but the woodwork has not been done, because the monastery does not have the money necessary for this, and the cells that were not affected by the fire more than suffice for the present number of monks.

Finally, a significant addition has been made to Xeropotamou's equipment: a petroleum operated machine for cutting timber. Facing economic difficulties, the monastery purchased this machine in order to reduce the expense of cutting and splitting the logs that are brought here from its forests. The machine introduced a discordant note to the quiet of the monastery, where the monks have been accustomed to hear not the irritating noise of machines, but the soothing melodies of Byzantine chant and the sweet song of birds. It is probable that since then this recent acquisition has been moved to the monastery's *arsanas* or landing place with warehouses and other buildings; for it is here that the timber is brought for shipment outside the Holy Mountain.

Chapter III

A RUMANIAN HERMIT

On a slope across from the Monastery of Xeropotamou, about ten minutes away, is the Kelli of the Dormition of the Theotokos, a dependency of the monastery. To reach it, one goes downhill and crosses the river from which the monastery got its name, which means, "monastery of the dry (*xeros*) river (*potamos*)," the river being dry during the summer.

The term kelli denotes both the cell of a monk and a monastic establishment consisting of a building with a chapel in it and some surrounding land and usually inhabited by three monks. The Kelli of the Dormition of the Theotokos is a cell in the second sense. When I visited it, I found one of the two monks who dwell there, Father Stephen. The other hermit was away on some chore. Stephen took me to the little chapel and then showed me the nearby fruit and vegetable garden. In the chapel I noted in particular the rather high iconostasis, reminiscent of the iconostases I have seen at the Russian Monastery, and the liturgical books, which are in Rumanian. Then we sat down and talked about life on the Holy Mountain, the Orthodox in general, and the state of mankind.

Father Stephen, a native of Rumania, speaks Greek fluently, but with a foreign pronunciation and at times incorrectly.

"I came here from Rumania when I was nineteen years old," he said, "and have remained here ever since, for fifty-seven years. I left Rumania accompanied by my grandfather. He came to the Holy Mountain as a pilgrim and departed after a week. My mother had died years before, and my father had given me his consent to come to the Mountain and become a monk.

"Our cell is self-sufficient, having a garden, vineyard, and five hundred olive trees. We have everything. Glory to God! All the other monks of Athos, too, have everything they need. The

99

All-holy Virgin (*Panaghia*) takes care of all of us."

Here was a person that was fully contented, a rare phenomenon among men, especially in the present age. He has attained contentment — one of the essential elements of true happiness — in a state which we in an "affluent society" would regard as great poverty. Completely free from cares about the material side of life, Stephen abides strictly by Christ's injunction: "Do not be anxious what ye shall eat, or what ye shall drink, or what ye shall put on."[1]

In connection with the hermit's last statement, it should be noted that Hagiorite monks speak of the Holy Mountain as "the Garden of the All-holy Virgin" Mary, and believe that it is under her special protection.

I was deeply impressed not only by the contentment of Father Stephen, but also by his meekness, serenity and dispassion. He listened to my account and that of another visitor about the unrest, strife and sin in contemporary society, and even about the apostasy of some prominent Orthodox prelates, without being disturbed. He remained serene, uttering no words of condemnation or indignation.

"There have always been wickedness in the world and scandals in the Church," he remarked calmly.

His manner of response was not a result of insensitivity to evil, such as that which William James finds in what he calls the "once-born," e.g. Walt Whitman. It was an expression of what the Orthodox Church Fathers call *passionlessness, (apatheia)*, which is freedom from anger, hatred, bitterness and all other negative emotions.

CHAPTER IV

ST. NICODEMOS' LAST ABODE

After leaving Father Stephen, I returned to the Monastery of Xeropotamou and took the path that leads to Karyes. A bus brought to Athos by the Greek government, some time after my previous sojourn, to help promote tourism, now runs daily from Daphne to that monastic village. It takes the bus half an hour to cover the distance from Xeropotamou to Karyes on the new zigzag road that was made by bulldozer, but close to two hours to cover by foot, proceeding on the old, direct narrow path. For ten drachmas (33 cents) the tourist now avoids the hardship of the long uphill walk. I preferred to go by foot.

At Karyes I procured a *Diamoneterion,* a kind of passport for the visitor of Athos issued by the central governing body of the Holy Mountain called the "Holy Community" (*Hiera Koinotes*), after registering at the office of the civil governor. Having been classified as an alien, I paid one hundred drachmas, twice the amount paid by those who are classified as Greeks. It might be noted that, accordingly as they wish, Greek government authorities have been classifying persons like myself, who were born of Greek parents outside of Greece, sometimes as "aliens" and sometimes as "Greeks."

When I received this official letter of admission to all the monasteries and their dependencies, I went to a cell at the edge of Karyes known as the Kelli of the Skourtaioi. I had read about this cell in the biographies of St. Nicodemos the Hagiorite and was eager to visit it. The cell is situated on an abrupt slope about a quarter of an hour southwest of the centrally located building of the Holy Community and the famous Church of the Protaton. It is surrounded by luxuriant vegetation, consisting of shrubbery and trees, particularly chestnuts; and has plentiful running water, a cistern, and a terraced garden that produces tomatoes, beans, cantaloupes, watermelons, grapes, and other vegetables and fruits. Despite these features, the place is not ideal for contemplative, physically inactive monks. The humidity is high and the cold extreme in the winter.

Two elderly Greek monks occupied the cell when I visited it. They were the Priestmonk Daniel, whose handicraft was tailoring, and Father Ananias, who did the farming. Like Stephen, the Rumanian hermit, they were contented with their mode of life, which combined regularly physical work and prayer.

Recently, I learned, Father Daniel died here after a short illness, at the age of sixty, and that Father Ananias broke one of his legs and was taken to a hospital at Thessaloniki, whence he returned healthy and sound. Ananias is now ninety-nine years old, yet very alert mentally, reads and writes with facility, and chants at the Monastery of Koutloumousiou, where he goes with the aid of a cane.

This cell is called the Kelli of the Skourtaioi because in Nicodemos' time its occupants were named Skourtaioi. These brothers esteemed the Saint very highly and often invited him to eat with them. Also, they supported him during his last years, when he still wrote incessantly, even though his health was failing. Nicodemos spent the last weeks of his life in their house, which survives to this day, receiving their constant loving care.

Father Daniel took me inside the two-storied house, offered a spoonful of preserve, a tiny cup of black coffee and a glass of water — the customary refreshments on Athos — and showed me the rather small room where Nicodemos is said to have spent his last days.

The holy skull of Nicodemos is treasured in a silver-covered case that leaves only a small part of the top exposed. It is kept in the chapel inside the house and is presented to Orthodox visitors for veneration. The chapel is dedicated to St. George. Its iconostasis is adorned with three icons of the Byzantine tradition — those of Christ, the Holy Virgin, and St. George — while on its icon stand (*proskynetarion*) there is a fine smaller icon of St. George done in the same style.

Few people come to this last abode of St. Nicodemos. But as his life and works become better known, the house of the Skourtaioi will become a shrine to be visited by all pilgrims to the Holy Mountain. Some day a chapel will be erected here in honor of Nicodemos. Since he was officially recognized as a Saint eighteen years ago, Fathers Daniel and Ananias have aspired to erect a chapel dedicated to him. But their lack of money made it impossible. Ananias believes that the necessary money will somehow be found, and hopes that before he passes on he will have the joy of seeing at least the foundations of the chapel being laid.[1]

CHAPTER V

RUSSIAN SKETE OF ST. ANDREW

A short distance north of Karyes is the large monastery-like Skete of St. Andrew. I visited it on my previous pilgrimages, but never succeeded in gaining access to the interior of its main church, which is dedicated to the Apostle Andrew. I found its doors locked and no one came to open them for me. The few surviving Russian monks who dwelt here paid no attention to visitors, going about their tasks as though the visitors were non-existent. This time I chanced to meet an aged Greek monk named Ilarion, "Hilary," who opened the church for me and led me about. Afterwards he took me to the guesthouse. No refreshments or food were offered, because there were only five monks in this skete, all of them aged, barely able to take care of themselves.

"At one time," said Ilarion, "there dwelt in this skete seven hundred monks. Today there are only five of us — four Russians and I. When all of us pass on, the skete will come under the direct administration of the Monastery of Vatopedi, of which it is a dependency."

With regard to the church, he remarked:

" The construction of the Church of St. Andrew was completed in 1880, and when it was consecrated there were present at the service many official persons who came from Russia specially for the occasion. Among them was Prince Alexis. But times change. Twenty years have elapsed when the last service was held in it."

The Church of St. Andrew is by far the largest on Athos. It approaches in size the great basilica of St. Demetrios at Thessaloniki. Architecturally it is not at all reminiscent of the latter, except in the use of the round arch and the division of the interior into five aisles. In general, its architecture is non-Byzantine, baroque. Though it is surmounted by a central dome, like most Byzantine churches, its facade brings to mind Gothic churches, having a high tower at the middle and two lower ones at the sides. The dome and other parts of the roof are surmounted by large onion-shaped projections with ornate crosses, a characteristic of Russian churches.

The division of its interior into five aisles is effected by means of pilasters, instead of round columns as in churches of the Byzantine order.

Unique on Athos is the floor of the edifice, being formed of boards that have been placed in such a manner that the lines of their edges form alternately upright and inverted V's, thereby creating the illusion of three-dimensionality, as though the floor were undulating like the sea. The effect, though rather striking, serves no religious function and in fact is distracting.

Quite impressive, too, is the iconostasis, which separates the holy bema from the rest of the church. It is very high and covered in its entirety with gold leaf. Unlike the iconostases of the Greek churches, which follow a straight line transversely, it has two curved projections, one between the Beautiful Gate and each of the side doors leading into the bema. Mounted on it are three tiers of icons, instead of the two observed in Greek churches. These icons as well as all the others of the church, many of which are plated with gold or silver, are typical of modern Russian iconography, inspired by Italian Renaissance models.

Having viewed both the exterior and the interior of the Church of St. Andrew, with its great size, undue complexity and showiness, one concludes that those who designed and decorated it were of a secular mentality, and sought rather to impress and dazzle the imagination of the beholder than to warm his heart and uplift his mind.

Recently, some noteworthy statements were made by Father Gabriel, abbot of the Monastery of Dionysiou, concerning the Skete of St. Andrew and its final complete desertion. He says:

"At the end of December, 1971, there departed to the Lord in extreme old age the last monk of the Russian Skete of St. Andrew the Apostle, named Sampson.

"The funeral service was held in the magnificent central church and there officiated the Director of the Athonias School, Archimandrite Chrysostom of the Monastery of Lavra, and Archimandrite Ambrose, a professor at the same school. It was attended by the members of the executive part of the Holy Community, representatives of the civil governor, and a great number of Fathers and laymen of Karyes. All were manifestly deeply touched by this sad end of the sacred institution, where until 1912 there dwelt 700 monks. . . .

"This Skete, formerly a Kelli, is a dependency of the holy Monastery of Vatopedi. When the Kelli was deserted, Vatopedi sold it to two Russian monks, who are regarded as the founders of the Skete. In 1845, the grand duke Constantine, second-born son of the Czar Nicholas I, put the foundation stone of the oldest Russian church in the Skete, that of the Holy Veil. And in 1867 the foundation stone of the stately Church of St. Andrew the Apostle was placed by the grand duke Alexis, uncle of Nicholas I. The church was consecrated in 1880. This buildng is 60 metres long, 33 wide, and 30 high. Its golden domes, its very tall bell-tower, and the surrounding many-storied buildings have given the skete a majestic appearance, and hence it is called the 'Kremlin of the East.' This famous Serayi ('Palace') . . . has been deserted; there reigns here the silence of death. Here, where incessant chanting used to be heard, there echo now the cries of noctural birds; here, where there shone gold and alabaster, spiders now perform their sinister work."

Gabriel mentions the chief events that led to the decline and end of monastic life at St. Andrew's. The first was the appearance of the factions of the "name-worshippers" and their critics. (The former were monks who practiced the Jesus Prayer — "Lord Jesus Christ, have mercy upon me" —, while the later were monks who either through misunderstanding or because of malice accused them of worshipping the name of Jesus instead of Jesus Himself.) Following a decision of the Synod of the Church of Russia, the "name-worshippers" were taken from the skete and brought by a steamer to the Caucasus, in May of 1913. The following year, when the First World War broke out, about 100 other, young monks were conscripted and brought to Russia via Bulgaria. From 1914 to the present day, not a single Russian has come to this Skete to become a monk, Russia having been cut off because of the Communist regime. The number of monks of the skete, diminishing each year as a result of deaths, reached the point of complete disappearance with the death of Father Sampson.

The Abbot of Dionysiou observes that the same plight now awaits another, older Russian skete, that of the Prophet Elijah. He says:

"Of the 300 monks it formerly had, there survive only 1 or 2. A sad state; and if the cursed-by-God Iron Curtain continues, something even sadder will take place, and the Pan-Orthodox character of Hagiorite Monasticism will change. May God, Who is All-Good, not allow this to happen."[1]

CHAPTER VI

MONASTERY OF KOUTLOUMOUSIOU

I went next to the Monastery of Koutloumousiou, which is but ten minutes southeast of Karyes, at a lower altitude. Here I was especially struck by the modernization of the guesthouse and the great decrease in the number of monks.

Significant even though not extensive, the modernization took place just prior to the celebration of the one thousand years of Athonite monasticism. Numerous persons from many nations came to the Holy Mountain in order to attend the special services, deliver speeches, or report the events in the press. Exploiting the occasion to promote its plan of gradually turning Athos into a tourist area, the Greek government introduced modern plumbing and other conveniences into the rooms and other parts of Koutloumousiou's guesthouse. Thus a modern sink and fountain were installed in each room, and a mirror was placed above them, thereby enabling tourists to shave and to groom themselves. Previously, there was only a large medieval fountain out in the long spacious corridor and no mirrors at all.

Those who judge by the criteria of Roman and modern aesthetics will applaud these new features. According to these, the hair that grows on a man's face is ugly and should unfailingly be scraped off completely every day. The monks, on the other hand, do not approve of these innovations, inasmuch as they never shave or use mirrors, and regard the mustache and beard as definitely becoming, enhancing the dignity of a man. They consider those visitors who shave while on Athos as showing disrespect for them and for the holiness of the place. In support of their conviction that the beard is becoming, they could cite the fact that the greatest aestheticians of ancient Greece, Plato and Aristotle, were bearded, as were the great poets and statesmen, such as Homer and Pericles. They could also quote St. Augustine, who asserts in *The City of God* that the beard adds to the beauty of the face.[1] But they are more likely to invoke the authority of St. Cosmas Aitolos, who led a life of spiritual endeavor on Mount Athos for many years. Cosmas viewed the beard as a badge of nobility for a Christian. In one of his *Didachai,* "Teachings," he says: "If there happens to be a man who is thirty years of age and has his beard, and there is another man who is fifty, or sixty, or a hundred and shaves, have the man who has his beard sit at a higher place than him who shaves, both at the church and at the table."[2]

As far as mirrors are concerned, the monks frown upon their use, regarding it as a form of narcissism and hence alien to the Christian way of life. Nicodemos the Hagiorite, it might be noted, devotes a whole section of his *Handbook of Counsel* to this subject, developing this point of view. He endorses the ironical statement, which he attributes to Plato, that a person should look into a mirror only when he is angry, so that seeing the ferocity of his face and the disorderly movements of his hands, he might feel shame and forsake such an irrational and mad passion.

When I visited Koutloumousiou in 1958, it had twenty monks. This time there were only seven. The invasion of Athos by tourism is undoubtedly the main direct cause of this sharp decrease in the number of monks. Tourism has especially affected Koutloumousiou, firstly, because of its proximity to Karyes, where all visitors to Athos have to go in order to register and obtain a letter admitting them to the monasteries, and secondly, because of the modernization of the guesthouse, making the guest rooms more like those of a modern hotel than are those of the small hotel in Karyes. The constant influx of tourists in the monastery, with the resultant distractions, has led the more contemplative monks to seek quieter, less distracting monastic establishments.

CHAPTER VII

MONASTERY OF GRIGORIOU

Returning to Daphne, I took the motorboat that carries passengers and supplies to the monasteries and sketes on the southeastern side of the peninsula. My destination was the Monastery of Grigoriou and other monasteries as well as the sketes of that area. The boat left Daphne at noon and arrived at Grigoriou in a little less than an hour, after stopping at the arsanas of the Monastery of Simonopetra. I noted that a new pier of concrete has been built here and a fine new storage building to replace the old one.

As one goes up the path that leads from the pier and small harbor of Grigoriou to the monastery itself, one is impressed by the great cleanliness and excellent maintenance of the whole arsanas and road.

When I and the other visitors arrived inside the courtyard, the guestmaster came and led us to the rooms where we were to rest and sleep.

Shortly after 3 o'clock the Ecclesiarch, a very dignified and reverend old monk, took the pilgrims to the main church and presented to them for veneration sacred relics of various saints, including Cosmas and Damian, Gregory the Theologian, Anastasia Pharmakolytria and others, and a small fragment of the Holy Cross.

On this occasion as well as later I had the opportunity to study the mural icons of the church. Those of the nave and the esonarthex are older than the wall paintings of the exonarthex. According to an inscription in the esonarthex, the former were done in 1779 by the hand of the hieromonk Gabriel, a native of Kastoria in northwestern Greece, while the latter are very recent, dating from 1962. Although the older murals are not done in the strict Byzantine style, they are inspired by Byzantine prototypes and are expressive of real piety. The recent ones, on the other hand, follow modern Russo-Italian models and are essentially unrelated to the

110

Orthodox spirit, being naturalistic and ostentatious in character. It is surprising that such works were done in this monastery, which is one of the best on Athos, at a time when Byzantine iconography has been extensively revived by the Orthodox and there are many good icon painters on the Holy Mountain who follow the Byzantine tradition of iconography.

During my two day visit at Grigoriou, I attended all the church services and was deeply moved by the very strict and devout manner in which they were conducted. The small vespers, which begin before sunset, took one hour. The compline commenced at early twilight. Its first part is held in the *liti* or inner narthex, the rest of it in the nave. As the service progressed, the church became almost totally dark, the only illumination being the feeble light provided by the sacred oil-lamps hanging before the panel icons of the iconostasis and elsewhere, and by the two oil-lamps of the chanters. This enhanced the mystical quality of the architecture, icons and hymnody, and evoked stronger religious feelings. The monks and guests were roused from bed for the orthros at 2:15 in the morning by the sounds first of the bells and then of the semantron. The lighting during this service was not much stronger than during the compline, being augmented only by the twin candle-like brass lamps on some of the chandeliers.

Grigoriou is a coenobitic monastery, governed by Abbot Vissarion, who is well-known and greatly respected on the Holy Mountain and far beyond its borders. He is of medium stature, somewhat heavy build, and has a big grey beard. His aspect is one of great serenity, inner strength and nobleness.

I talked with Father Vissarion in his office about Hagiorite monasticism and the state of Orthodoxy in the world. Among the questions I asked was what he thought of the view expressed recently in a book by Archimandrite Augustine Kantiotis (now Metropolitan of Phlorina) that Hagiorite monks should become more active in missionary work throughout Greece following the example of St. Cosmas Aitolos.

"I am all for such missionary work," said Vissarion. "But how can Athos produce missionaries when the number of monks has been growing smaller? We need more monks. A few years ago there were forty monks at this monastery, now there are only thirty. Further, we need more *learned* monks. St. Cosmas, it should be remembered, was a learned man. Our problem is how to attract more brothers to the Mountain, especially how to attract and train monks who combine great learning with great piety. Also, it should be realized that something more than learning and piety is needed for successful missionary work: there must be a call from God, as there was in the case of Cosmas."

Archimandrite Vissarion's eagerness to do more in the way of missionary work than his occasional talks outside of Athos found effective expression in the establishment by him in 1964 of the periodical *Saint Gregory*.[1] Published by this monastery, *Saint Gregory* contains excellent edifying articles and poems, mainly by Athonite monks, and is sent gratis to numerous persons and institutions in Greece and abroad. Its purpose is both to edify the Orthodox who live in "the world," and to attract worthy men to the monasteries of the Holy Mountain by criticizing anti-monastic ideas and practices, and presenting the monastic ideal in its true light. I will quote from a characteristic editorial on present day anti-monasticism:

"The monastic ideal has not ceased strongly to attract select souls. There exist, yes, there exist today monastic tendencies. There are souls which in the midst of all material goods, and of all the fascinations of the world, do not find repose. But they do find repose at some secluded holy Monastery. How is this to be explained? The world is perplexed and astonished when it sees some person withdraw to a Monastery — a person who could live in society with every material comfort. But it would not have been perplexed and would not have been astonished, if it had a 'Christly mind.'

"The world, however, is not simply perplexed and astonished. The world is aroused and organizes a whole expedition when a soul makes the heroic decision to lead the monastic life. Countless beings take the road towards disgraceful sin, towards the dens of Satan, and the world is not moved at all. A single being takes refuge in a Monastery, and the whole world is mobilized to seize it like a hawk, and to throw it again outside the Monastery. What is saddest is that even Religious and Ecclesiastical figures become persecutors of the Monastic life. They, too, become the world. . . . Instead of praising those rare souls, who in our unbelieving and pleasure-seeking epoch manifest the heroism to follow the life of self-denial, they struggle with every means to cool their zeal and turn them away from their holy decision. . . ."[2]

After our discussion on monasticism, I asked Father Vissarion what he thought of the 'ecumenism' of Patriarch Athenagoras. He replied:

"I do not approve of it at all, and have written him pleading that he stop it, because it involves performing acts that are contrary to the holy canons of our Church and making pronouncements that imply apostasy from the Orthodox Faith. Others on the Holy Mountain have written similar letters. But he does not answer any. We for our part have ceased commemorating him at the Divine Liturgy."

Archimandrite Vissarion stressed that the action of the Monastery of Grigoriou was directed not against the Patriarchate of Constantinople as such, but against the anti-canonical and more broadly un-Orthodox actions of this occupant of the Patriarchal throne.

Of great interest in this connection are also some remarks which Vissarion makes in a 1967 issue of the periodical of the monastery. Thus he says:

"The Holy Mountain is today in agony and in a state of commotion from one end to the other, as a result of the rash leaps of the Patriarch. We mean his declarations that 'nothing separates us from the Latins,' that 'the dogmas will be placed in the store-room,' that 'the union will take place and let the Theologians continue their dialogues,' and that 'Theology equals love;' and what is most shocking of all, the fact that he has been taking part in prayers and Doxologies with the non-Orthodox and allows them to bless the Orthodox faithful as if they (the non-Orthodox) were Orthodox clergymen, thereby trampling upon the Holy Canons.

"Patriarch Bekkos, too wanted to bring about a union of the Orthodox with the Latins through joint prayers and liturgies. He,

too, spoke in the name of love. And he came to the Holy Mountain
and burned and destroyed; and we have the hosiomartyrs of the
Holy Mountain who suffered martyrdom when he was Patriarch.
At the Protaton of the Holy Mountain there is an ever-burning
sacred lamp before the graves of these saints. There is a similar
sacred lamp at the cenotaph of the Holy Monastery of Zographou.

"The universal demand on the Holy Mountain today is the
same: The Ecumenical Patriarch must stop prayers with the heterodox; and he must stop his unionist declarations. Orthodoxy has her
arms open to every heretic who wishes to be saved: let him draw
near."[3]

CHAPTER VIII

MONASTERY OF DIONYSIOU

From the Monastery of Grigoriou I went by foot to that of Dionysiou. It took me two hours. The path that connects these monasteries is very narrow, running through dense shrubbery, and alternately uphill and downhill. During my stay at Dionysiou I had the opportunity to converse with the abbot Archimandrite Gabriel, the librarian and secretary Father Theocletos, and Fathers Dositheos and Ilarion.

I met Ilarion soon after I entered the monastery. A conversation with him started when he learned that I was from the United States.

"I am eighty years old," he said. "I have been here for thirty years and lived in Pittsburgh for twenty-eight."

"Why did you come to the Holy Mountain?" I asked.

"I came here because I saw the sins and vanity of worldly life," he replied.

Father Ilarion speaks and writes English with facility, though not faultlessly. He made a strong impression on an English officer, W. B. Thomas, during the Second World War, and is mentioned in the latter's book *Dare to be Free*, which was published in 1951 at London. Thomas stayed at Dionysiou for nine days during the German occupation of Greece. He was saved from the Germans by the fathers of this monastery at the risk of their own lives. They sent him by rowboat to the Monastery of Lavra, whence he went to Turkey and then to Egypt.

Not long after our first meeting, Father Ilarion came to my room in the guesthouse and gave me a small sheet of paper on which he had written in English, under the heading "Memorandum," the following:

"When back to Boston remember to write to the Editor of

Saturday Review to send you a copy of the *Saturday Review* of March 14, 1964. Read the article 'Mount Athos.' Write to Pittsburgh Press to send you a copy of his paper March the 15th, 1964. Read the article 'Road to Damascus,' with two full pages in pictures. — Father Ilarion, Dionysiou Monastery, Daphne, Agion Oros, Greece."

With Archimandrite Gabriel, then seventy-nine years old, I talked about the "ecumenism" of Patriarch Athenagoras and about Orthodox monasticism. He spoke in his customary serene, meek, yet firm manner. Like Vissarion, he was definitely opposed to the "ecumenical" activities and pronouncements of the Patriarch, and regarded them as detrimental to the Orthodox Church and not serving the true spiritual interests of other churches. He remarked that his stand on this matter has been formally stated in a proclamation that was published in the periodical *Hagioreitike Bibliotheke,* "Hagiorite Library," and the newspaper *Orthodoxos Typos,* "Orthodox Press." His name appears first at the end of the proclamation and is followed by the names of many other greatly respected monks of Athos. This historic document bears the title "Proclamation of Hagiorite Fathers to the Orthodox Greek People," and states:

"The Hagiorite Fathers — Abbots, Hiermonks, and Monks — whose names appear below, having learned of the recent machinations against our Orthodox Faith by the Papal Insurrection and the unionist slogans of the Ecumenical Patriarch and his collaborators, proclaim with a stentorian voice that we denounce such unionist slogans and unionist tendencies, and abide firm and unshakable by our Orthodox Faith, following what has been prophesied by the God-inspired Prophets and has been taught by the Heralds of God, the Apostles, by the God-bearing Choir of Fathers, by the Seven Ecumenical Synods and by the Local Synods, having as our head the Corner-stone Christ, our God, and in a word abiding by all that our Orthodox Faith teaches, either through writing or through Tradition, and rejecting "Union" or "Unity," as the unionists lately have been calling it.

"If the Catholics and the other heterodox want to return to Orthodoxy, let them come themselves repenting and asking for compassion, espousing fully the dogmas and the Tradition of our blameless Orthodox Faith. It is not proper for us the Orthodox to run to them.

"We make an appeal to the Ecumenical Patriarch to stop his unionist activities, for if he continues them we shall disavow him.

"Furthermore, we declare that we shall struggle for our Orthodoxy until our last breath, shedding our very blood if need be, imitating our ever memorable Predecessors, crying out with Joseph Vryennios: 'We will not forsake you, our beloved Orthodoxy; we will not deny you our traditional holiness; we will not withdraw from you, O Mother Piety; in you we were born, in you we live, and in you we shall die.'

"We congratulate the venerable Archbishop of the Orthodox Church of Greece (Chrysostomos) and all the Orthodox Hierarchs of Greece for their vigorous stand on behalf of our Orthodoxy, and declare that we are by their side.

"The Holy Mountain, January 23(O.S.), 1964."[1]

Turning to the subject of monasticism, I asked Father Gabriel some questions about his recently published book, *The Monastic Life According to the Holy Fathers.*

"I wrote it," said Gabriel, "prompted by the appearance of several anti-monastic books, particularly one by the Metropolitan Philip of Drama, in which he asserts that contemporary Orthodox monasticism serves no purpose and should be reorganized in the direction of social service, and thus become like early monasticism, which according to him served orphanages and homes for the aged. In my book I criticize this view."

Here are some of the things Father Gabriel says in the Introduction of his book in criticizing this position:

"Monastic life is a Divine call, an aspiration for devotion to God, and an endeavor of man to attain as far as possible perfection in Christ, according to the statement of the Lord in the Gospel: 'If thou wantest to become perfect, renounce everything and come and follow me.' The Church Fathers regard the Monastic life as a service to God which is absolute, and they call it *angelic*. They regard it as embracing, first, the love of God, and through it the love of neighbor so far as possible.

"If the Fathers wanted Monasticism to be 'a social servant,' they would not have hastened to the desert, but would have headed for the cities, where there was such need, especially in those days, when there was no organized social service either on the part of the State or on the part of the Church.

"Nowhere in their writings do the Fathers of our Church exhort the monks to social service, but advise avoidance of the world, self-concentration, dedication to the love of God and the keeping of His commandments through strict bodily and spiritual purity.

"Basil the Great, par excellence the teacher and organizer of Eastern Orthodox Monasticism, by word and deed advises monks to withdraw from the world, and to have as their mission an entirely exemplary life, so that through it the monastic life might be praised and the name of God be glorified. He did not recommend social activity and philanthropic work even for the convents for women, which then flourished in Cappadocia and Pontus. Nor is there any mention anywhere that in the philanthropic institutions which he established he appointed monastics for any service whatsoever.

"Although it does not have an aversion for altruism, Orthodox Monasticism has for its mission, as I said, devotion to God, love towards Him in the first place, and in the second place love towards men, which it practices in relation to monastics, especially within brotherhoods, and towards pilgrims and visitors who come to the holy monastic establishments. . . .

"From the beginning, Eastern Orthodox Monasticism has sat by the feet of Jesus, like Mary, whom the Lord called blessed, and in silence and humility has listened to His words. By contrast, Western Monasticism follows the work of Martha, 'troubling itself about many things,' in the midst of the world and of noisy society.

"The views of recent years calling for a change of direction in our monastic life, instead of benefiting it, harm it seriously. For man can practice philanthropy and religious social work without the monastic ideal and habit. Thus young men are indirectly dissuaded from monasticism. . . . Further, these views influence many young monks, who owing to their superficial knowledge accept them as an argument, return to the world in order to offer their supposed services to the public and the Church, and most of them suffer shipwreck through their inexperience on the reefs of today's sly and hypocritical society."[2]

From Father Theocletos I heard a critical evaluation of the Brotherhood of Theologians "Zoe." Several group leaders (*kyklarchai*) of this brotherhood happened to be visiting the monastery, and this led to a discussion of it. "Zoe" is one of the most influential religious organizations in Greece, having representatives all over the country, a weekly journal, and numerous books authored by its members, sold in its own and other bookstores. In his critique, Theocletos said:

"Zoe has been doing considerable good work. It has been providing valuable religious instruction and moral training to the people — a task which the official Church has not been performing at all adequately. But the scope of Zoe's teaching and spirituality is rather restricted. Beyond these there is the great spiritual wealth of the Eastern Church Fathers, whom the Zoe theologians are only now beginning to discover. And beyond the 'good works' of the members of this brotherhood there is spiritual purification (*katharsis*), without which good works are useless. Thus, the theologians of Zoe have tended to interpret the Holy Scriptures in accordance with what some minor theologian, belonging to Zoe, has written, whereas we ought to follow the interpretation of the holy Fathers. Also, like the Roman Catholics, the members of Zoe attach much importance to good works in the 'world.' But such works of themselves do not lead to salvation. We must learn to regard our good works as nothing. And we must learn to regard our spiritual attainments as nothing, by looking up to the perfection which we lack.

"The Zoe Brotherhood has improperly been characterized as monastic. It has in fact been anti-monastic. The anti-monasticism of Zoe has been one of the reasons why young men do not come to Athos to become monks. When I came to this monastery twenty years ago there were seventy monks; now there are only thirty-five. Monasticism must be given due recognition, not only as a legitimate way of life, but as the only way that leads to the highest spiritual attainments. In the 'world' the attainment of perfection is impossible."

With Father Dositheos, an elderly monk whom, like Ilarion, I met for the first time, I talked about the mode of life practiced at the Monastery of Dionysiou. He summed up thus what he regarded as its main features:

"We fast, stay up at vigil services, pray, repent, confess, and partake of Holy Communion. Constant care of the soul is necessary, if we are to attain salvation."

This account is quite consonant with that given by Abbot Gabriel in his book *The Holy Monastery of Saint Dionysiou on the Holy Mountain.*

"The brothers of this holy monastery, today as in the past, 'owing nothing to anyone' except to love God and their neighbor and one another, cleanse themselves through fasting, prayer and confession, and otherwise lead a life worthy of their calling, and thus render their holy monastery worthy of every respect."[3]

CHAPTER IX

SKETE OF ST. ANNE

Bypassing the Monastery of St. Paul, which is the next one after Dionysiou as one proceeds along the southern side of the Athos peninsula towards its outer end, I went by motorboat to the *arsanas* of the Skete of St. Anne, in order to go up to the skete and attend the feast in commemoration of the Dormition of St. Anne—the mother of the Theotokos—to whom the main church of this settlement of hermits is dedicated. This skete, the largest on Athos, is built on an abrupt slope a good distance from the sea. To reach its main church, known as the *kyriakon,* where the monks of the settlement gather on Sundays and other holy days for corporate worship, I had to walk uphill for about half an hour.

The all-night vigil service, which constituted the heart of the celebration, was one of the most memorable experiences I have had on the Holy Mountain. It began at 8 o'clock in the evening of August 6 (July 24 O.S.) and continued until 8:30 in the morning, when the Divine Liturgy, which followed the great vespers and matins, ended. This service had a spiritual magnificence that moved one profoundly, evoking contrition and a strong feeling of the presence of God. The chanting was done by two choirs, each consisting of three monks, all of them having beautiful voices and well-trained in the execution of Byzantine music. They stood in stalls along the east wall of the nave that is in line with the iconostasis, and faced west towards the congregation. At the beginning of the service the church was dark, illumination being provided only by the small sacred oil-lamps in front of the icons of the iconostasis. When the right choir began to chant Psalm 140 (Septuagint): "Lord, I have cried unto Thee; hear me: attend to the voice of my supplication. . .," one of the monks lit the candles of the great chandelier (under the dome) known as the "corona," those of the three other chandeliers in the nave, and those before the icons of the iconostasis, in front of the Beautiful Gate, and elsewhere. Thus the intensity of the illumination gradually increased until the whole nave became well illuminated. It was a warm, pulsating light, unlike the lifeless light provided by electricity. The sacred figures depicted on the panels and walls now became visible, increasing the feeling of holiness and contact with the divine. This feeling was further strengthened by the frequent censing with the famed Athonite frankincense.

When the priest said in a loud intoned voice: "With fear of God, with faith and with love draw near," many of the monks and lay guests moved forward to the Beautiful Gate to partake of Holy Communion.

After the Liturgy, food was offered in the refectory to all who had attended the services. The meal consisted of fish soup, boiled fish, cheese, whole wheat bread, and wine. This was not the only hospitality provided to the guests. Upon their arrival at the skete the previous evening, they were all offered refreshments in the reception room by the *Dikaios* or Prior of the skete or by his assistant. These included loukoum, coffee, and water.

When the meal was over, one of the monks of the Skete of St. Anne, a retired Metropolitan named Anthimos, delivered a moving speech, in which he related the celebration to the goals of monasticism. The chief purpose of this event, he asserted, is to lift us to God and His saints, and to arouse our zeal to imitate Sts. Anne and Joachim, to strive to acquire their virtues, to rid ourselves of "passions" (negative emotions) and evil thoughts, to cleanse our soul of everything impure, so that we might attain happiness in the other, endless life, and so far as possible in the present life also.

CHAPTER X

THE NEW SKETE

From St. Anne I went to the New Skete. This lies near the sea, northwest, in the direction of the Monastery of St. Paul, of which it is a dependency. It took me twenty minutes of downhill walking to reach it. Here the Dikaios led me to a room of the guesthouse where I was to stay for the night, and then to the Kalyva of the Haldezoi or Haldaioi, where I was to be a guest in the evening.

The cottage has been named after its previous elder, whose surname was Haldezos. This monk came here from Plomari, Lesvos, at an early age, and died a few years before my visit, at the age of ninety-five. The present elder of the kalyva, Father Dorotheos, is a native of Adramiti, Asia Minor. Dorotheos offered me a liberal supper, and we conversed on various subjects, including fishing, which is his special manual skill.

The Haldaioi brotherhood consists of four monks. Dorotheos is considerably older than the others, two of whom are icon painters while the other performs various chores. Iconography is the chief means of their sustenance. Additional means, besides fishing, are one hundred olive trees, some lemon and orange trees, and a vegetable garden.

Early the next day I attended the Divine Liturgy held in the central church of the skete. It commenced at 6 o'clock and went on for an hour and a half. Prior to the Liturgy, an elderly monk read in the esonarthex a very edifying homily from one of the Sunday Sermonaries (*Kyriakodromia*) by Nikephoros Theotokis, eminent 18th century Greek bishop, theologian and educator. The subject was the wrong, perverted forms of anger, desire, faith and hope, and their good forms. Theotokis' Sunday Sermonaries, which consist of commentaries and homilies on the excerpts from the Gospels, Epistles of Paul and Acts of the Apostles that are read in

Orthodox churches during the Liturgy on Sundays, are among the
favorite books of the monks of Athos. It was the first time, however, that I heard one of his homilies read to a congregation.

After the Liturgy, the following ceremonial is observed at this
skete. The monks and any lay pilgrims that happen to be in the
church go forward before the Beautiful Gate, receive *antidoron*,
"holy bread," from the priest, kissing his hand, then kiss the icon
on the icon stand in the south side of the nave, and next the icons
on the iconostasis, beginning from the south end and proceeding
towards the north end. After this, each one takes some *kollyva*
(specially prepared boiled wheat), if there are any in commemoration of a particular saint or deceased monk.

Upon leaving the church, all the monks and guests went to
the nearby reception room. Here, the traditional Athonite refreshments were offered, and there was an informal discussion on various
religious subjects. There came up what was then the most discussed
topic on Athos, that of the efforts of Patriarch Athenagoras to unite
the Orthodox Church with the Roman Catholic, and whether he
should be commemorated in the services. The prevailing view here
as elsewhere on the Mountain was that he had proved clearly by his
words and by his deeds that he was no longer an Orthodox Christian, and hence he should not be commemorated.

Later in the day I went to the kalyva of Hieromonk Ephraim,
spiritual son of the saintly elder Joseph the Hesychast, who reposed
here in 1959.[1] When I first met Ephraim in 1958, he lived alone in
a hut some distance from Father Joseph's. Now he was the head of
a group of eight young monks.

"There were two more brothers," remarked this young priest-
monk, "but a few days ago their fathers according to the flesh came
and snatched them away with wrath and violence. However, I believe they will soon return. Two others are about to join us and
become monks, one of them a microbiologist."

In order to accommodate all these monks, Father Ephraim en-
larged considerably the house of his departed elder and made a large
terraced vegetable garden.

The handicraft of this brotherhood is making prayer ropes

(*komboskoinia*) for monks and laymen, and small, beautifully carved wooden crucifixes depicting Christ crucified on one side and the Theotokos and the Child Christ on the other. They are all in great demand. But the production of these articles, especially of the crosses, is a slow process, because all the work is done very carefully and by hand.

Since my visit in 1965, Father Ephraim's group has increased to twenty. He needed larger living quarters and found suitable ones at a deserted Russian kelli at Provata.

What accounts for Ephraim's extraordinary success in attracting so many men to monasticism, at a time when there are numerous anti-monastic forces operating in the world? It is, above all, his purity and holiness. And this he owes in large measure to his elder Joseph. For, as St. Gregory of Nyssa remarks, "the saintliness of a life is transmitted from him who has achieved it to those who come within his circle; for there is truth in the Prophet's saying, that one who lives with a man who is holy and clean and elect will become such himself."[2]

CHAPTER XI

MONASTERY OF ST. PAUL

My sojourn on the Holy Mountain ended with a visit to the Monastery of St. Paul. This is one of the best coenobia today, and one of the very few monasteries where the number of monks increased since my previous visit. In 1958 it had forty brothers, this time it had forty-six. Many of them, including the officiating priest, are young. The rather aged abbot, Archimandrite Seraphim, whom I met in 1958, had died a year or two later. He was succeeded by a middle-aged monk, Father Andreas.

The diet at St. Paul's is healthful, containing plenty of vegetables grown near the monastery, and whole wheat bread made of flour ground by the monastery's own mill.

In connection with the subject of health, I talked with an elderly father regarding the physical state of the monks of the Holy Mountain. He remarked that as a rule it is good. Heart trouble, he observed, is very rare. He added that the most widespread ailment is rheumatism, owing to the high humidity of the region. This monk has been here continuously for forty-seven years and never had occasion to leave Athos for medical care.

I had a longer conversation with the librarian, Father Theodosios, a very kindly and cheerful elderly monk. I talked with him especially about the periodical *St. Paul of Xeropotamou*,[1] of which he was the editor. He attributed to the appearance and wide circulation of this periodical the growth of the number of monks at St. Paul's. This edifying journal first appeared in 1950, and ceased to be published in 1964, when the Monastery of Grigoriou began to publish *Saint Gregory*, which is quite similar to it in scope and format.

Just recently, Father Theodosios published a valuable book, entitled *The Heavenly Manna: The Treasure which is Ignored by*

126

Most Persons.[2] He wrote it moved by the desire to enlighten both clergy and laymen about the great importance of frequent Communion as a means of attaining freedom from "passions," of arousing the aspiration after the virtues and making progress in them, and of attaining union with God. Also, he hoped to correct various misconceptions regarding this Mystery, such as the belief that one must receive Holy Communion only four or five times a year and must always fast for three successive days before receiving it. Theodosios makes reference to passages in the New Testament, to the canons of the Ecumenical Synods, and to statements made by numerous early and later Church Fathers and by many Orthodox religious writers of modern times. This book brings to mind the Kollyvades movement on Athos in the 18th century,[3] and is bound to provoke much discussion there and elsewhere among the Orthodox.

I noted that the upkeep of the Monastery of St. Paul is excellent. Cleanliness and order are seen everywhere. Quiet prevails throughout it. Strictness is emphasized in all matters pertaining to belief and practice, and is beautifully exemplified in the life of this holy brotherhood.

CONCLUDING POSTSCRIPT

During the last four decades, there has been much speculation and concern about the survival of monasticism on the Holy Mountain, prompted by (a) the reduction of the number of monks, (b) the anti-monastic spirit of our age, and (c) the invasion of Athos by tourism. The most pessimistic note was sounded in 1934 by the sociologist Michael Choukas of Dartmouth College, in his book *Black Angels of Athos*. Considering the future of Athos on the basis of the data he had gathered there, and in the light of sociological theory, Choukas wrote: "The end is not far. . . . To predict that this will happen within the next generation is hazardous — not because it may not happen, but because it may occur sooner."[1] Taking the span of a generation to be thirty-three years, monasticism on Athos should have come to an end at the very latest by 1967. But this has not happened. Although the number of monks on Athos has decreased considerably since the time when Prof. Choukas' book was published, Athonite monasticism survives, and survives with considerable vigor.

We have noted that the Russian Skete of St. Andrew closed in 1971, and that a similar fate seems to await the Russian Skete of the Prophet Elijah.[2] We have also noted that the number of monks at the Monastery of Koutloumousiou has dropped sharply in recent years. In 1958 I found twenty; in 1965, only seven. There has also been a sharp decline in the number of monks at the Russian Monastery, Panteleimonos. In 1958 there were eighty-five monks at Panteleimonos; in 1972, according to a report, there were only seventeen.[3] On the other hand, in the case of the Serbian Monastery, Hilandari, the number of monks has gone up slightly. When I visited it in 1958, there were twenty-five monks; in 1971, according to a report, there were twenty-six.[4] At the Monastery of St. Paul,

128

I found more monks in 1965 than in 1958: their number had grown from forty to forty-six. The Skete of St. Basil, which is in one of the most inaccessible regions of the Holy Mountain, had only three monks about half a century ago; now it has eight.

No official figures about the number of monks at each monastery or the total number of monks on Athos are available. The latter is estimated to be about fifteen hundred. In connection with the drop in the number of brothers at some of the monasteries since my earlier sojourn on Athos, it should be pointed out that in many instances this has resulted from the departure of monks to a skete or other hermitage, either in order to avoid being continually distracted by tourists, or to avoid worship in churches where the late Patriarch Athenagoras was commemorated.

The closing down of a monastery or skete because its last inhabitant has died or gone elsewhere does not necessarily mean the final end of it as a place of monastic life. Thus, the Russian Kelli of St. Artemios at Provata, which was long deserted, was recently reinhabited by twenty Greek monks under Hieromonk Ephraim,[5] disciple of Joseph the Hesychast. Also, the Monastery of Stavronikita, which closed in 1968,[6] because there were no more monks there, opened soon afterward. Archimandrite Basil Gontikakis, a graduate of the School of Theology of the University of Athens, was appointed abbot of Stavronikita by the Holy Community of Athos, and was joined by several other pious monks.[7] The appointment of an abbot means that this monastery is now coenobitic, whereas previously it was idiorrhythmic. Thus the temporary closing down of the Monastery of Stavronikita turned out to be not a disaster, but an opportunity for inaugurating there a stricter mode of monasticism. (With this change, the number of Athonite monasteries that follow the coenobitic system has risen from eleven to twelve. This means that now only eight monasteries on Athos follow the idiorrhythmic system.)

With regard to the vanishing Russian population of the Holy Mountain, it should be remarked that the worse seems to be over. In the fall of 1972, five Russian monks were admitted to the Monastery of Panteleimonos.[8] They were the first monks to be admitted from Russia since the Bolshevik Revolution more than fifty years ago. According to a report, when the Patriarch of Moscow Pimen visited Athos last fall, the abbot of Panteleimonos asked him to send there three hundred monks.[9] It is not to be expected that this request will be fulfilled in the near future. But it does seem likely that henceforth small groups of Russian monks will, from time to time, be allowed entry to Athos, to settle at the Monastery of Panteleimonos and at the deserted Russian sketes.

The anti-monastic mentality of our time, which was discussed in the chapters on the monasteries of Grigoriou and Dionysiou, is obviously closely related to the reduction in the population of the Holy Mountain. If this mentality should change, if a more enlightened attitude towards Eastern Orthodox monasticism should prevail, the population of the Mountain can definitely be expected to rise. That this might happen is not only possible, but even very likely. The growing number of publications that are intended for monks and persons interested in Orthodox spirituality provides ground for such an expectation. Thus, during the last fifteen years there have appeared in Greece a new, five-volume edition of the *Philokalia,* a new, four-volume edition of *Evergetinos,* and new editions of the *Ladder* of St. John Climacos, both in the original Greek and in modern Greek paraphrase, of the *Extant Works of St. Symeon the New Theologian,* of the *Ascetic Works* of St. Isaac the Syrian, of the *Lausaikon,* the *Gerontikon,* or "Book of the Elders," and many other works that present the methods, ideals and wisdom of Eastern Orthodox monasticism. The circulation of such works will help create an intellectual climate favorable to monasticism. That such a climate has already been forming is evinced by the recent spreading and prospering of women's monasticism in many parts of Greece, both in the mainland (e.g. Attica, Kozani) and in the islands (e.g. Chios, Lesvos).

The other major danger to Athos that has been mentioned, tourism, also causes much concern to the monks of Athos, for it disrupts their solitude, their quiet, and places a heavy burden on the monasteries, which provide free meals and refreshments as well as clean linen to all visitors. Tourism is seen by the monks as an influx of the "world," which they have sought to leave behind. The result is that in proportion as tourism increases, the Holy Mountain loses, for those who have monastic tendencies, the fascination which it has had until recent years, as a region apart from the "world" of multiform distractions and passions.

Of the three dangers which I have discussed, the first — the reduction in the number of monks — is regarded by the Athonites as the most fearful. But these pious and determined men believe that they will confront this danger, as well as the others, successfully. Thus, in 1963, on the occasion of the celebration of the one thousand years of organized monastic life on Athos, Father Theocletos of Dionysiou remarked: "The Holy Mountain will always remain as it is, a place of repentance, of purification and of incessant praising of the Lord, and a Monastic Center that continues the ancient monastic tradition of the Orthodox Church."[10] More recently, Archimandrite Evdokimos, abbot of the Monastery of Xenophontos, speaking about the dangers that I have discussed, said: "With the help of God and the intercessions of our Lady Theotokos, we shall confront all the dangers victoriously."[11]

This conviction, which is typical of the monks of Athos, and the spiritual vitality within Athos today, manifested by their publications, by what they said in conversations I had with them, by their vigorous reaction to anti-monastic ideas and acts, and to misconceived Orthodox ecumenism, and also by the revival of mental prayer and the stress on other spiritual practices — all these things together provide the strongest assurance that monasticism on Athos will go on, will survive until the end of time.

Strong assurance about this is also provided by the high esteem in which Athos has been held by many prominent Greeks, whose thought has exercised and continues to exercise much influence in Greece, where the Athos peninsula lies. Thus, Eleftherios Venizelos (1864-1936), the greatest modern Greek statesman, has remarked: "The Greek state and the Greek people as a whole look at the Holy Mountain as to the Ark of our religious and national traditions."[12] Referring to the anti-monastic spirit of our age, Venizelos observed: "The changed mentality of the world does not look at monastic life as it was viewed in earlier centuries; but the Holy Mountain has exceptional reasons (for continued existence), and we are internationally bound, and it is to our national interest, to preserve monastic life there."[13]

Writing in the same spirit, Basil Laourdas (1912-1971), well-known philologist and for many years director of the Institute for Balkan Studies at Thessaloniki, has said: "We must preserve intact the presence of the Holy Mountain as a spiritual power, as the Greek people have preserved it intact for one thousand years. And we must hand it over intact to the generations that will come."[14]

Fotis Kontoglou (1895-1965), renowned icon painter and writer, has spoken of Athos as "a priceless treasure, something unique in the world, . . . where everything is calm and sanctified, where men find spiritual consolation, become holy and pray day and night for mankind."[15] Kontoglou never had doubts that Athonite monasticism would survive, despite the widespread materialism, unbelief and anti-monasticism of our time.

Finally, to give one more example, Nicholas Louvaris (1887-1961), who was professor of theology and philosophy of religion at the University of Athens, and member of the Academy of Athens, has spoken eloquently of the great importance of Athos and expressed his confidence that monasticism would survive there. In his book *Athos: The Gate to Heaven,* Louvaris says: "The fear of an impending dissolution of the Holy Mountain is unjustifiable. The resoluteness of the monks guarantees the opposite. 'The miraculous is the beloved child of faith,' and miracles of the preservation and revival of Athos have taken place often down to this day, thanks to the faith and the resolution of the monks. Moreover, the thinning of the ranks of precisely a community that has refused to base itself on a materialistic world-view will lead many men to a mustering of their spiritual resources, to a return to the soul, and therefore to a revival of religiousness. This means that sooner or later many will again be turning to the path that leads to the hermitages of Athos. Besides, flight from the world is a need of the soul that forms one of the perennial types of human life. In conclusion, the preservation of Athos is guaranteed also by the consciousness of the Greek Nation that is turned towards Byzantium. Athos par excellence symbolizes Byzantium, whose spirit, art, and legends have been piously guarded by the Hagiorites through the centuries."[16]

NOTES

PART ONE

SCHOLARS, MISSIONARIES, AND SAINTS

CHAPTER I

Scholars

1. *Hyper ton Hieros Hesychazonton,* in Migne, *Patrologia Graeca,* Vol. 150, col. 1116.

2. *Logos peri Nepseos kai Phylakes Kardias.*

3. Regarding the *Philokalia,* see my books *Byzantine Thought and Art* (1968), Chapter IV, and *Modern Orthodox Saints,* Vol. 2, *St. Macarios of Corinth* (1972), pp. 23-25, 96-101.

4. *Logos ten en Christo Ergasian Diasaphon kai Deiknyon en Brachei tou Monadikou Epangelmatos ton Kopon.*

5. *Gregoriou tou Palama Syngrammata,* ed. by Panayotis Christou and others. Thessaloniki, Vols. 1-3, 1962, 1966, 1972. Among recent works that deal with Palamas are: Vasilii Krivosheine, *The Ascetical and Theological Teaching of Gregory Palamas,* in *Eastern Churches Quarterly,* 1938, No. 4, and London, 1954; Georges Florovsky, "Saint Gregory Palamas and the Tradition of the Fathers," in *The Greek Orthodox Theological Review,* Vol. 5, No. 2, Winter, 1959-1960; John Romanides, "Notes on the Palamite Controversy," in *Greek Orthodox Theological Review,* Vol. 6, No. 2, Winter, 1960-1961; John Meyendorff, *A Study of Gregory Palamas,* London, 1964; and George C. Papademetriou, *Introduction to Saint Gregory Palamas,* New York, 1973.

6. Vol. 154. Migne has published some other writings by Philotheos, mainly in Vol. 151.

7. Since this was written, Prof. B. L. Dentakis, of the School of Theology of the University of Athens, published (in 1972) for

the first time from the codices of Athos the life and akoluthia of Philotheos, together with an informative introduction about him, and indicated that he plans to publish this saint's unpublished works pertaining to hesychasm.

8.   *Methodos kai Kanon syn Theo Akribes peri ton Hairoumenon Hesychos Bionai kai Monastikos.*

9.   *Peri Proseuches.*

10.   Quotation in the Brief Biography of these monks contained in the Greek *Philokalia.*

11.   *Maximos ho Graikos.*

12.   *Nea Hellas,* "Modern Greece," Athens, 1872, p. 159.

13.   *Hamartolon Soteria.* Venice, 1641.

14.   *Hagios Kosmas ho Aitolos,* "Saint Cosmas Aitolos," 3rd ed., Athens, 1966, pp. 152-153.

15.   See e.g. *The Way of a Pilgrim,* trans. by R. M. French, New York, 1952, pp. 138-139.

16.   Styl. S. Bairaktaris, *Agapios Landos ho Kres,* "Agapios Landos the Cretan, Athens, 1970, pp. 26-27.

17.   Venice, 1643.

18.   Venice, 1641.

19.   Venice, 1644.

20.   Venice, 1656.

21.   Bairaktaris, *op. cit.,* p. 27

22.   Venice, 1685

23.   Venice, 1657.

24.   Venice, 1643.

25.   Cf. Constantine Sathas, *Neohellenike Philologia,* "Modern Greek Philology, Athens, 1868, p. 313.

26.   *Lausaikon tou Hagiou Orous,* Volos, 1953, p. 10.

27.   *Hermeneia tes Zographikes Technes,* ed. by A. Papadopoulos-Kerameus. Petroupolis (Petrograd), 1901.

28.   Paris, 1845.

29.   Appendix II (pp. 263-399) of *Christian Iconography; or, The History of Christian Art in the Middle Ages,* by Adolphe Napoleon Didron, translated from the French by E. J. Millington,

and completed with additions and appendices by Margaret Stokes. London, 1886. Reprinted in 1965 at New York.

30. This was written in Moldavian and first appeared in print in 1803. A Greek version, *Anatrope tes Threskeias ton Hebraion,* was published at Jassy in 1818.

31. *Proskynetarion tou Hagiou Orous.* Venice, . . .

32. *Kata Kalviniston.*

33. *Encheiridion Anonymou Tinos peri tou hoti Chreostousin hoi Christianoi Sychnoteron na Metalambanousi ta Theia Mysteria.* Venice, 1777.

34. *Sylloge Panton ton Hieron kai Theion Kanonon.* Venice, 1787.

35. See my book *St. Macarios of Corinth,* pp. 15-31.

36. *Peri ton O' Hermeneuton tes Palaias Theias Graphes,* "Concerning the 70 Translators of the Divine Old Scripture," Vol. 4, Athens, 1849, p. 821.

37. *Scholia eis ton Thoukydiden.*

38. *Scholia eis ta Ethika tou Aristotelous.*

39. *Philosophos e Theistes.*

40. *Theodorou Grammatikes Eisagoge ton eis Tessara eis to Tetarton Hypomnema.* Bucharest, 1768.

41. *Op. cit.,* p. 497.

42. A manuscript of this work is kept at the Monastery of Iviron and another at the Monastery of Xenophontos. See Zaviras, *op. cit.,* pp. 325-326.

43. *Kepos Chariton,* "Garden of the Graces," Athens, 1880, p. 49.

44. *Logos tou en Hagiois Patros hemon Kyrillou Alexandrias peri Exodou Psyches kai Peri tes Deuteras Parousias.* Venice, 1763.

45. *Margaritai ton Trion Hierarchon, etoi Logoi Parainetikoi Metaphrasthentes eis to haploun.* Venice, 1779.

46. *Enkolpion Logikon, toutestin Hymnoi eis ten Panymneton Theotokon kai Euchai dia Stichon Diaphoron Metron te kai Melon.* Venice, 1770.

47. *Exegesis tes Theias Leitourgias.* Venice, 1795.

48. *Katalogos Historikos.*

49. *Dakikai Ephemerides.*
50. Paris, 1888.
51. *Kathreptes Gynaikon,* 2 vols. Leipzig, 1766.
52. Elias P. Voutieridis, *Syntome Historia tes Neohellenikes Logotechnias,* "Brief History of Modern Greek Literature," 2nd ed., Athens, 1966, p. 208.
53. *Exomologetarion.* Venice. 1794.
54. *Aoratos Polemos.* Venice, 1796.
55. *Neon Martyrologion.* Venice, 1799. See my book *St. Macarios of Corinth,* pp. 32-35, 85-95.
56. *Gymnasmata Pneumatika.* Venice, 1800.
57. *Pedalion.* Leipzig. 1800.
58. *Symbouleutikon Encheiridion.* Vienna, 1801.
59. *Hagios Nicodemos ho Hagiorites.* Athens, 1959.
60. *Akolouthia tou Hosiou kai Theophorou Patros hemon kai Didaskalou Nikodemou tou Hagioreitou.* "Akoluthia of our Holy and God-bearing Father and Teacher Nicodemos the Hagiorite," Mount Athos, 1955, p. 15.
61. *Mikron Proseuchetarion.* Venice, 1828.
62. *Synopsis.* Aegina, 1831.
63. *Horologion to Mega.* Venice, 1832.
64. Venice, 1836.
65. Venice, 1839.
66. Constantinople, 1843.
67. *Ho Athos,* "Athos," Constantinople, 1885, p. 234.
68. *Adamantes tou Paradeisou.*
69. *Peri Synechous Metalepseos.* Athens, 1886, 1895.
70. Athens, 1898.
71. *Proskynetarion tou Hagiou Orous tou Atho.*
72. *Neos Euergetinos.* Volos.
73. A monumental work of over a thousand folio pages, containing the teachings and instructive incidents from the lives of hundreds of Desert Fathers. It was first published in 1783 in Venice, after it was edited by Nicodemos the Hagiorite. See my book *St. Macarios of Corinth,* pp. 24-25, 31-32.
74. *Lausaikon tou Hagiou Orous.* Volos, 1953.

75. P. 8.

76. *Phone Boontos ek tes Eremou.* Volos, 1955.

77. *Malthousianismos, e to Englema tes Genoktonias.* Volos, 1957.

78. *Anamneseis kai Nostalgiai.* Thessaloniki, 1958.

79. *He Hiera Mone tou Hagiou Dionysiou.* Athens, 1959.

80. *He Monachike Zoe kata tous Hagious Pateras.* Athens, 1962.

81. *Hodegos Pneumatikou kai Exomologoumenou.* Athens, 1971.

82. *Metaxy Ouranou kai Ges.* Athens.

83. *Hagios Nikodemos ho Hagioreites.* Athens, 1959.

84. *Athonika Anthe.* Athens, 1962.

85. *Seminarium Kondakovianum,* No. 8, pp. 99-154.

86. *The Eastern Churches Quarterly,* 1938, No. 4.

87. Paris, 1963-1965.

88. *The Christian East,* 1952, pp. 35-50.

89. *Orientalia Christiana Periodica,* 1954, pp. 298-328.

90. E.g. some edifying chapters have been published in the periodical *Hosios Gregorios,* "Saint Gregory," 1966 (March-April), pp. 434-440. On Dionysios, see Manuel Gedeon, *op. cit.,* pp. 210-211.

91. *Kosmos kai Psyche.*

92. *Logoi kai Paraineseis tou Hosiou Patros hemon Ephraim tou Syrou eis haplen phrasin Metaglottisthentes, kai Merikoi Bioi Hagion Tinon.* Venice, 1721.

93. *Hodegos, e Eisagoge eis tas Theias Graphas.* Aegina, 1831.

94. *Enkolpion, e Spoudasma kata ton Antipheromenon enantion tes Theotokou kai tou Timiou Stabrou.* Nauplion, 1832.

95. *Anaskeue tou Bibliariou kata tes Katagoges tou Propatorikou Amartematos.* Constantinople, 1835.

96. *Didaskalia Christianike, e Katechesis.* Athens, 1841.

97. *He Eremetes Photine.*

98. *Biographike Skiagraphia tou en Hosiois Aeimnestou Patros hemon kai Poimenarchou Nektariou, Metropolitou Pr. Pentapoleos.* Athens, 1929. English translation by Constantine Cavarnos

in *The Orthodox Word,* Vol. 2, No. 2, 1966.

99.   *Hagios Paulos ho Xeropotamitis.*

100.   *To Ouranion Mana.* Volos, 1969. See below, Part Three, Ch. XI.

101.   Paris, 1952; London, 1958.

102.   *Ho Hagios Nektarios: Ho Hierarches, ho Logios, ho Asketes.* Athens, 1970.

103.   *Dialogoi tes Eremou Peri Oikoumenismou.* Athens, 1971. More recently, Father Theodoretos published a book entitled *He Eucharistiake Symmetoche en Hagio Orei,* "Participation in the Eucharist on the Holy Mountain." Athens, 1972.

104.   See C. Sathas, *Neohellenike Philologia,* p. 297.

105.   See my book, *Modern Orthodox Saints,* Vol. 1, *St. Cosmas Aitolos,* 1971, pp. 26, 61.

106.   See my book *St. Macarios of Corinth,* pp. 15-32, 39, 49-50.

107.   See *St. Macarios of Corinth,* pp. 25-26, *et passim.*

108.   See Sathas, *op. cit.,* p. 622.

109.   Kontoglou went to Mount Athos twice, and was profoundly influenced by its iconography and spirituality. See his *Histories kai Peristatika,* Athens, 1944, pp. 18-23, my book *Byzantine Sacred Art* (1957), pp. 44-56, and my article "Fotis Kontoglou," in *The Orthodox Word,* Vol. 2, No. 4, 1966, p. 136.

110.   Leontiev made two pilgrimages to the Holy Mountain. The first time he stayed there for three weeks; the second, for over a year. He attributed great importance to these sojourns. Thus he wrote: "I went to Mount Athos in order to learn to become a true Orthodox Christian, in order that the austere monks might teach me to believe" (Nicholas Berdyaev, *Leontiev,* Orono, Maine, 1968, p. 63). Also, he remarked: "The essentials of my works are to be found in what I wrote after 1872; that is, after my pilgrimages to Mount Athos, and after my return to personal Orthodoxy;" and: "My best works (the *Odyssey* and *Byzantinism and Slavdom*) were written after a year and half of communion with the monks of Athos" (*ibid.,* pp. 61, 64).

Chapter II

Missionaries

1. Libertyville, Illinois, 1951.
2. Quoted by M. Gedeon, *op. cit.,* p. 205.
3. *The Orthodox Word,* September-October, 1968, pp. 187-206.
4. Constantin de Grunwald, *Saints of Russia,* London, 1960, p. 91.
5. New York, 1950.
6. New York, 1960.
7. Vol. 2, Cambridge, Mass., 1966.
8. *Neon Martyrologion,* 3rd ed., Athens, 1961, p. 60.
9. P. 61.
10. This is contained, in English translation, in my book *St. Cosmas Aitolos.*
11. *Neon Martyrologion,* pp. 202, 203.
12. *Kosma Aitolou Analytike Bibliographia* (1765-1967). Athens, 1968.
13. C. Cavarnos, *St. Cosmas Aitolos.*
14. P. 61.

Chapter III

Saints

1. *Akolouthia ton Hosion kai Theophoron Pateron hemon ton en to Hagio Orei tou Atho Dialampsanton.*
2. *Hagiologion tes Orthodoxou Ekklesias.* Athens, 1960.
3. *Op. cit.,* p. 317.
4. P. 316.
5. *Philokalia,* Vol. 5, Athens, 1963, pp. 104-105, 107.

6. Evlogios Kourilas, Lavriotis, *Historia tou Asketismou*: *Athonitai*, "History of Asceticism: Athonites," Vol. 1, Thessaloniki, 1929, pp. 122-123.

7. *Ibid.*, pp. 121-122.

8. Venice, 1803.

9. Evlogios Kourilas, *op. cit.*, p. 78.

10. *Ibid.*, p. 80.

11. See note 6 above.

12. October, 1959, pp. 343-344.

13. *Ho Bios tou Aeimnestou mas Patros Ioseph tou Hesychastou*, New Skete, 1962.

Epilogue

1. *Klimax*, Constantinople, 1883, p. 84; cf. St. John Climacus, *The Ladder of Divine Ascent*, trans. by Archimandrite Lazarus Moore, New York, *c.* 1959, p. 144.

2. Cf. C. Cavarnos, *Byzantine Thought and Art*, pp. 27-28.

PART TWO

MUSIC, MUSICIANS, AND HYMNOGRAPHERS

CHAPTER I

Music

1. Saint Basil, *The Letters*, Loeb Classical Library, Vol. 1, New York, 1926, Letter 2, p. 13.

2. W. K. L. Clarke, *The Ascetic Works of Saint Basil*, London, 1925, Rule XXXVII, p. 206.

3. G. I. Papadopoulos, *Symbolai eis ten Historian tes par' Hemin Ekklesiastikes Mousikes*, "Contributions to the History of Our Church Music," Athens, 1890, pp. 235-236; Alice Gardner, *Theodore the Studite*, London, 1905, p. 242.

4. Alice Gardner, *op. cit.*, p. 80.

5. Amos, 5: 23.

6. 2nd ed., Athens, 1961, p. xviii. Cf. C. Cavarnos, *Byzantine Sacred Music,* 1956, 1966, pp. 18-19.

7. London, 1936, p. 56.

8. Cf. D. G. Panagiotopoulos, *Theoria kai Praxis tes Byzantines Ekklesiastikes Mousikes,* "The Theory and Practice of Byzantine Ecclesiastical Music," Athens, 1947, p. 302.

9. *Philokalia, Vol.* 4, Athens, 1961, p. 9.

10. *Ibid.,* p. 226.

11. *Ibid.,* p. 10.

12. G. I. Papadopoulos, *op. cit.,* pp. 100-101.

13. *Pedalion,* "The Rudder," Athens, 1957, p. 286.

14. *Kepos Chariton,* "Garden of Graces," Volos, 1958, p. 11.

15. *Chrestoetheia ton Christianon,* "Christian Morality," 2nd ed., Syros, 1838, p. 288.

16. *Ibid.,* p. 21.

17. *Philokalia,* Vol. 4, p. 14.

CHAPTER II

Musicians and Hymnographers

1. P. 231. There are about 2,200 Byzantine music manuscripts in the libraries of Mount Athos. How many of these are by monks of Athos remains to be determined. A young Greek theologian and musicologist, Gregory Stathis, has made them an object of painstaking study since 1970, and plans to publish them under the sponsorship of the Foundation for Byzantine Musical Studies of the Church of Greece. See *Ekklesia,* November 1-15, 1972, pp. 626-629, Dec. 1-15, pp. 694-698, Jan. 1-15, 1973, pp. 50-53.

2. Cf. G. I. Papadopoulos, *Historike Episkopesis tes Byzantines Ekklesiastikes Mousikes,* "Historical Survey of Byzantine Church Music," Athens, 1904, pp. 74-75.

3. P. 240.

4. *Contributions to the History of Our Church Music,* p. 266. Cf. his book referred to in note 2 above, p. 78.

5. See Papadopoulos, *Contributions,* p. 276. Cf. Zaviras,

Modern Greece, p. 312: "He was a very wise, very saintly, very theological man. . . . He appears to have flourished in the 16th century. . . . His enchiridion entitled *Thekaras* contains hymns and prayers in praise of the most laudable and indivisible Trinity — Father, Son, and Holy Spirit. . . . This book is small in size, but is far greater in quality than most others (not to say than all others) of this type."

6. K. A. Psachos, *He Parasemantike tes Byzantines Mousikes,* "The Notation of Byzantine Music," Athens, 1917, p. 36; *Threskeutike kai Ethike Enkyklopaideia,* "Religious and Ethical Encyclopedia,' Athens, 1962-1968, Vol. 6, cols. 516-517.

7. See the Encyclopedia mentioned in the preceding note, Vol. 11, col. 1126.

8. Papadopoulos, *Contributions,* p. 276.

9. *Ibid.,* p. 278.

10. *Ibid.,* p. 306.

11. *Ibid.,* p. 310.

12. *Synkrisis tes Arabopersikes Mousikes pros ten Hemeteran Ekklesiastiken.*

13. Papadopoulos, *Contributions,* pp. 310-314; Psachos, *op. cit.,* p. 36.

14. *Ibid.,* p. 311; Psachos, *op. cit.,* p. 74.

15. Papadopoulos, *Contributions,* pp. 312-313.

16. *Ibid.,* pp. 307-308. The akoluthia, in honor of Sts. Barnabas, Sophronios and Christophoros, was published in 1769 at Bucharest and in 1775 at Leipzig (Sophronios Eustratiadis, *Hagiologion tes Orthodoxou Ekklesias,* "Hagiology of the Orthodox Church," Athens, 1960, p. 72).

17. Papadopoulos, *op. cit.,* pp. 308-309.

18. *Ibid.,* p. 326; Zaviras, *op. cit.,* pp. 553-554.

19. Papadopoulos, *op. cit.,* pp. 440-441.

20. *Ibid.*

21. *Apolytikia, Kontakia, kai Magalynaria.* Athens, 1957.

22. See my book *Anchored in God,* pp. 196-197.

23. *Athos,* p. 331.

PART THREE

RECENT VISIT TO ATHOS

CHAPTER I

On The Way

1. See my article *Nikon ho Hagiorites,* "Nikon the Hagiorite," in the periodical *Kibotos,* "The Ark," July, 1953, pp. 260-262, and *Anchored in God,* pp. 190-192.

CHAPTER II

Monastery of Xeropotamou

1. The basis of this time system is sunset: when the sun sets it is twelve o'clock, the hour immediately after is one o'clock, the next hour is two, and so on.

CHAPTER III

A Rumanian Hermit

1. Matt. 6: 25.

CHAPTER IV

St. Nicodemos' Last Abode

1. After this was written, a committee of friends of Mount Athos was formed in Athens to raise money to this end. The response has been excellent, and the erection of a chapel dedicated to Nicodemos will probably commence in the very near future.

CHAPTER V

Russian Skete of St. Andrew

1. *Orthodoxos Typos, "Orthodox Press,"* March 15, 1972, p. 2.

CHAPTER VI

Monastery of Koutloumousiou

1. Bk. XXII, Ch. 24.
2. Augustine N. Kantiotis, ed., *Ho Hagios Kosmas ho Aitolos*, "Saint Cosmas Aitolos," 2nd ed., Athens, 1959, p. 86.

CHAPTER VII

Monastery of Grigoriou

1. *Hosios Gregorios.*
2. January-February, 1968, pp. 949-950.
3. November-December, pp. 854-855.

CHAPTER VIII

Monastery of Dionysiou

1. *Hagiorite Library*, March-April, 1964, pp. 133-134. This proclamation, followed by a great many more names, reappeared in the May-June issue of *Hagiorite Library*, pp. 161-164.
2. *Op. cit.*, pp. 4-6.
3. P. 142.

CHAPTER X

The New Skete

1. See above, Part One, Ch. III, Sect. 6.
2. *On Virginity*, Ch. 24.

CHAPTER XI

Monastery of St. Paul

1. *Hagios Paulos ho Xeropotamites.*
2. *To Ouranion Manna: Ho dia tous Pollous Egnoemenos Thesauros.* Volos, 1969.
3. See my book *St. Macarios of Corinth*, pp. 15-31.

Concluding Postscript

1. *Black Angels of Athos,* Brattleboro, Vermont, 1934, p. 296.

2. See Part Three, Ch. V.

3. *Orthodoxos Typos,* "Orthodox Press," November 15, 1972, p. 8.

4. *Ekklesia,* May 1-15, 1971, p. 271.

5. See Part Three, Ch. X.

6. *Ekklesia,* September 1, 1968, p. 415.

7. *Ekklesia,* October 1, 1968, p. 476.

8. *Orthodoxos Typos,* November 15, 1972, p. 8.

9. *Ibid.*

10. *Ekklesia,* August 1-15, 1963, p. 386.

11. *Orthodoxos Typos,* August 10, 1970, p. 3.

12. *Ekklesia,* August 1-15, 1963, p. 398.

13. *Ibid.*

14. Periodical *Gregorios Palamas,* March-April, 1963, p. 145.

15. *Histories kai Peristatika, "Stories and Incidents,"* Athens, 1944, pp. 18-19.

16. *Athos: He Pyle tou Ouranou,* 2nd ed., Athens, 1962, p. 101.

APPENDIX A

MENOLOGIUM OF ATHONITE SAINTS

The names of the saints are ordered according to the month and day when their memory is celebrated. In general, the date is that when the saint died. All the Athonite saints are commemorated together on the Sunday after the Sunday of all Saints. As September first is the beginning of the ecclesiastical year, I have commenced the Menologium by listing the saints who are specially commemorated this month. In the case of those saints who are discussed in this book, I have inserted in parentheses the Part, Chapter, and the Section in which they are discussed.

SEPTEMBER

13. HIEROTHEOS THE YOUNGER, hosios, of Iviron. 1686-1745. (Pt.I, Ch. I, Sect. 18.)
14. MACARIOS, hosiomartyr, of Dionysiou. A disciple of St. Niphon, Patriarch of Constantinople. Suffered martyrdom in 1507 at Thessaloniki. (Pt. I, Ch. II, Sect. 4.)

    JOSEPH, hosiomartyr, of Dionysiou. Suffered martyrdom in 1819 at Constantinople.
20. ILARION, hosiomartyr, of the Skete of St. Anne. Suffered martyrdom in 1804 at Constantinople.
22. TWENTY-SIX HOSIOMARTYRS OF ZOGRAPHOU, who censured the Latinizing Emperor Michael Palaiologos and Patriarch Bekkos, and were burned alive in 1285 in the tower of the Monastery of Zographou by Latins and Latinizers. (Pt. I, Ch. III, Sect. 1.)

    COSMAS THE BULGARIAN, hosios, of Zographou. D. 1323

OCTOBER

1. JOHN KOUKOUZELIS, hosios, of the Monastery of Lavra. 12th century. (Pt. II, Ch. II, Sect. 1.)
   GREGORY, hosios, Domestikos of Lavra. A contemporary of Koukouzelis. (Pt. II, Ch. II, Sect. 1.)
5. EVDOKIMOS, hosios, of Vatopedi.
6. MACARIOS, hosiomartyr, of the Skete of St. Anne. Was beheaded in 1590 at Brusa.
8. IGNATIOS, hosiomartyr, of Iviron's Skete of Prodromou. Was hanged in 1814 at Constantinople.
   PHILOTHEOS, Patriarch of Constantinople, hosios. C. 1300-c. 1379. (Pt. I, Ch. I, Sect. 4, Pt. II, Ch. II, Sect. 5.)
15. EUTHYMIOS THE YOUNGER, hosios. Dwelt on Athos as a hermit. 823-899.
21. PHILOTHEOS, hosios, of Dionysiou. D. 1610.
26. JOASAPH, hosiomartyr, of Dionysiou. A disciple of St. Niphon, Patriarch of Constantinople. Suffered martyrdom in 1518 at Constantinople. (Pt. I, Ch. II, Sect. 5.)
28. ATHANASIOS THE YOUNGER, Patriarch of Constantinople, hosios. He was a monk at the Monastery of Esphigmenou before he became Patriarch of Constantinople. As Patriarch he served between 1289-1293, and 1303-1311.
29. TIMOTHY, hosiomartyr, of Esphigmenou. Suffered martyrdom in 1820 at Adrianople.

NOVEMBER

1. IAKOVOS, hosiomartyr, of Iviron's Skete of Prodromou. Suffered martyrdom in 1520 at Adrianople together with his disciples hosiomartyr IAKOVOS, deacon, and hosiomartyr DIONYSIOS, monk. (Pt.I, Ch. II, Sect. 7.)
9. EUTHYMIOS, hosios, founder of the Monastery of Docheiariou in the latter part of the 10th century.
   NEOPHYTOS, hosios, uncle of Euthymios and co-founder of the Monastery of Docheiariou.
12. NILOS THE MYROBLYTE, hosios, of Lavra. D. 1651.

13. DAMASKINOS, hosiomartyr, of Lavra. Suffered martyrdom in 1681 at Constantinople.
    DAMIAN, hosiomartyr, of Lavra.
14. GREGORY PALAMAS, Archbishop of Thessaloniki, hosios. 1296-1369. Also commemorated on the Second Sunday of Great Lent. (Pt. I, Ch. I, Sect. 3.)
17. GENNADIOS, hosios, of Vatopedi.
22. CALLISTOS XANTHOPOULOS, hosios. D. 1363. (Pt. I, Ch. I, Sect. 5.)

D E C E M B E R

3. COSMAS, hosiomartyr, of the Skete of St. Anne. Suffered martyrdom at Constantinople.
5. NECTARIOS, hosios, of the Kelli of Iagri near Karyes. D. 1406.
   PHILOTHEOS, hosios, of Karyes. A spiritual guide of St. Nectarios.
   HOSIOMARTYRS FROM THE KELLIA OF KARYES who censured the Latinizing Emperor Michael Palaiologos and Patriarch Bekkos. One of these, the *Protos* of Athos, was hanged; the rest were killed by sword.
7. GREGORY, hosios, founder of the Monastery of Grigoriou about the middle of the 14th century.
26. CONSTANTIOS THE RUSSIAN, hieromartyr, of Lavra. Suffered martyrdom in 1743 at Constantinople.
28. SIMON THE MYROBLYTE, hosios, founder of the Monastery of Simonopetra towards the middle of the 14th century.
30. GEDEON, hosiomartyr, of the Monastery of Karakallou. Suffered martyrdom in 1818 at Tyrnavos, Thessaly.

J A N U A R Y

4. EUTHYMIOS, hosiomartyr, abbot of the Monastery of Vatopedi. Suffered martyrdom in 1285 for censuring for their error the Latinizers Emperor Michael Palaiologos and Pa-

triarch John Bekkos. (Pt.I, Ch. III, Sect. 1.)

TWELVE HOSIOMARTYRS OF VATOPEDI, who suffered martyrdom in 1285 together with their abbot Euthymios for censuring the Latinizing Emperor and Patriarch. (Pt. I, Ch. III, Sect. 1.)

ONOUPHRIOS, hosiomartyr, deacon of the Monastery of Hilandari. Suffered martyrdom in 1818 in Chios.

5. ROMANOS, hosiomartyr, disciple of St. Akakios Kafsokalyvitis. Suffered martyrdom in 1694 at Constantinople. (Pt. I, Ch. III, Sect. 5.)

6. MACARIOS MAKRIS, hosios, a monk at Vatopedi and later abbot of the Monastery of Pantocratoros at Constantinople. D. 1431.

11. THEODOSIOS, hosios, abbot of the Monastery of Philotheou and later Metropolitan of Trebizond. Died *c.* 1392.

13. MAXIMOS KAFSOKALYVITIS, hosios. Died *c.* 1320. (Pt. I, Ch. III, Sect. 4.)

14. SAVA, hosios, founder of the Monastery of Hilandari and first Archbishop of Serbia. 1169-1235. (Pt. I, Ch. II, Sect. 2.)

16. DAMASKINOS, hieromartyr, of Hilandari. Suffered martyrdom in 1771 at Gambrovo, Bulgaria.

21. NEOPHYTOS, hosios, prosmonarios of Vatopedi.
MAXIMOS THE GREEK, hosios, of Vatopeli. *c.* 1470-1556. (Pt. I, Ch. I, Sect. 6.)

24. DIONYSIOS OF OLYMPOS, hosios, abbot of the Monastery of Philotheou. 16th century.
PHILOTHEOS, hosios, founder of the Monastery of Philotheou towards the end of the 10th century.

FEBRUARY

13. SYMEON, hosios, founder of the Monastery of Hilandari. 1113-1199. (Pt. I, Ch. II, Sect. 2.)

23. DAMIAN, hosios, of the Monastery of Esphigmenou. D. 1280.
DAMIAN, hosiomartyr, disciple of St. Dometios of the Monastery of Philotheou. Suffered martyrdom in 1568 at Larissa. (Pt. I, Ch. II, Sect. 8.)

MARCH

1. AGAPIOS, hosios, of Vatopedi.
22. EUTHYMIOS, hosiomartyr, of Iviron's Skete of Prodromou. Suffered martyrdom in 1814 at Constantinople. Also commemorated on May 1.
23. LUKE, hosiomartyr, of the Skete of St. Anne. Suffered martyrdom in 1802 at Mytilene.

APRIL

4. THEONAS, hosios. Dwelt at the monasteries of Pantocratoros and Simonopetra, and later became Archbishop of Thessaloniki. D. c. 1545.
6. GREGORY BYZANTIOS, hosios, of the Monastery of Lavra. D. 1308.
   GENNADIOS, hosiomartyr, of the Monastery of Dionysiou. Suffered martyrdom in 1818 at Constantinople.
12. AKAKIOS THE YOUNGER, hosios, founder of the Skete of Kafsokalyvia. D. 1730. (Pt. I, Ch. III, Sect. 5.)
16. CHRISTOPHOROS, hosiomartyr, of Dionysiou. Suffered martyrdom in 1818 at Adrianople.
    NIKETAS, hieromartyr, of the Skete of St. Anne. Suffered martyrdom at Serrai.
19. AGATHANGELOS, hosiomartyr, of the Monastery of Esphigmenou. Suffered martyrdom in 1819 at Smyrna.
    SYMEON, hosios, abbot of the Monastery of Philotheou. 16th century. (Pt. I, Ch. II, Sect. 9.)

MAY

1. EUTHYMIOS, hosiomartyr, of Iviron's Skete of Prodromou. Suffered martyrdom in 1814 at Constantinople. Also commemorated on March 22.
   IGNATIOS, hosiomartyr, a fellow spiritual striver of St. Euthymios. Suffered martyrdom in 1814 at Constantinople. Also commemorated on October 8.

AKAKIOS, hosiomartyr, a fellow spiritual striver of Sts. Euthymios and Ignatios. Suffered martyrdom in 1815 at Constantinople.

4. NIKEPHOROS THE SOLITARY, hosios. Died *c.* 1300. (Pt. I, Ch. I, Sect. 1.)

7. NILOS THE MYROBLYTE, of Lavra. D. 1651. Also commemorated on November 12.

NIL SORSKY, OR NILUS OF SORA, hosios. (Part I, Ch. II, Sect. 2.)

PACHOMIOS, hosiomartyr, disciple of St. Akakios the Younger of Kafsokalyvia. Suffered martyrdom in 1730 at Ushak of Philadelphia, Asia Minor. (Pt. I, Ch. III, Sect. 5.)

13. JOHN THE IBERIAN (i.e. Georgian), hosios, founder of the Monastery of Iviron.

EUTHYMIOS THE IBERIAN, hosios, son of St. John the Iberian and founder of Iviron. D. 980.

GEORGE THE IBERIAN, hosios, cousin and biographer of St. Euthymios the Iberian.

GABRIEL, hosios, of Iviron. Finder of the icon of the Holy Virgin "Portaitissa" in the sea.

HOSIOMARTYRS OF IVIRON who suffered martyrdom by being thrown into the sea by the Latinizers for censuring the error of Emperor Michael Palaiologos and Patriarch Bekkos.

22. PAUL, hosiomartyr, of Lavra and the Russian Monastery. Suffered martyrdom in 1818 at Tripolis of the Peloponnesos.

JUNE

12. PETER THE ATHONITE, hosios, one of the first hermits of Athos. Fl. 9th century.

14. NIPHON, hosios, disciple of St. Maximos Kafsokalyvitis. D. 1330. (Pt. I, Ch. III, Sect. 4.)

18. LEONTIOS THE HAGIORITE, hosios of Dionysiou. D. 1605.

20. CALLISTOS XANTHOPOULOS, Patriarch of Constantinople, hosios. Dwelt at Iviron's Skete of Magoula before he

was ordained Patriarch. D. 1363. (Pt. I, Ch. I, Sect. 5.)

25. DIONYSIOS THE HAGIORITE, hosios, founder of the Monastery of Dionysiou in 1375.

DOMETIOS, hosios, fellow spiritual striver and friend of St. Dionysios the Hagiorite, and abbot of the Monastery of Dionysiou for fifteen years. D. 1405.

PROCOPIOS, hosiomartyr, of the Skete of Iviron. Suffered martyrdom at Constantinople.

26. DAVID, hosiomartyr, of the Skete of St. Anne. Suffered martyrdom at Thessaloniki.

J U L Y

3. GERASIMOS, hosiomartyr, of the Skete of Panteleimonos, a dependency of Koutloumousiou. Was beheaded in 1812 at Constantinople.

5. ATHANASIOS THE ATHONITE, hosios, founder of the Monastery of Lavra in 963. (Pt. I, Ch. III, Sect. 3.)

CYPRIAN, hieromartyr. Dwelt at the Kelli of St. George of the Monastery of Koutloumousiou. Suffered martyrdom in 1679 at Constantinople.

8. THEOPHILOS THE MYROBLYTE, hosios. Dwelt at the Kelli of St. Basil of the Monastery of Pantocratoros. Died in 1548.

9. DIONYSIOS THE ORATOR, hosios, first settler of the Small Skete of St. Anne. D. 1606. (Pt. I, Ch. I, Sect. 18.)

METROPHANIS, hosios, disciple of St. Dionysios the Orator.

10. ANTONY PECHERSKY, hosios, of Esphigmenou, founder of the Cave Monastery near Kiev. D. 1073. (Pt. I, Ch. II, Sect. 1.)

NICODEMOS THE ALBANIAN, hosiomartyr, of the Skete of St. Anne. A disciple of St. Akakios the Younger. Suffered martyrdom in 1722 at Albasan, Albania. (Pt. I, Ch. III, Sect. 5.)

NECTARIOS, hosiomartyr, of the Skete of St. Anne. Suffered martyrdom in 1820 at Smyrna.

14. NICODEMOS THE HAGIORITE, hosios. 1749-1809. (Pt. I, Ch. I, Sect. 12.)

26. GERONTIOS, hosios, first settler of the Skete of St. Anne.

28. PAUL XEROPOTAMITIS, hosios, founder of the monasteries of Xeropotamou and St. Paul in the 10th century.

A U G U S T

7. DOMETIOS, hosios, of the Monastery of Philotheou. 16th century

11. NIPHON, Patriarch of Constantinople, hosios. Dwelt at the Monastery of Dionysiou before he became Patriarch and afterward. 1425-1515. (Pt. I, Ch. II, Sect. 2.)

18. SOPHRONIOS, hosios, of the Skete of St. Anne.

ARSENIOS THE YOUNGER, hosios. Dwelt on the Holy Mountain for six years with his Elder Daniel, and there received the "Great and Angelic Habit." He reposed at the Holy Transfiguration Monastery in Paros on January 31, 1877, at the age of seventy-seven.

19. THEOPHANES, hosios, of the Monastery of Docheiariou. 16th century.

24. COSMAS AITOLOS, hieromartyr and peer of the Apostles. Suffered martyrdom at Kalkoutas, near Berati, Albania. 1714-1779. (Pt. I, Ch. II, Sect. 11.)

Apolytikion Chanted in Honor of
All the Saints of Mount Athos

"Let us honor with hymns and odes the Fathers of Athos, angels who were invested with bodies—Confessors and Ascetics, Hierarchs and Martyrs—imitating their virtues, and chanting in unison: Glory to Him Who crowned you. Glory to Him who sanctified you. Glory to Him Who rendered you our guardians, protecting us from dangers."

APPENDIX B

GLOSSARY

Akoluthia. (Greek *akolouthia,* pl. *akolouthiai.*) A Church service, such as the orthros, the Divine Liturgy, the vespers, or a special service in honor of a saint. An akoluthia in honor of a saint comprises many hymns, all of which are chanted, and often includes an account of his life.

Apodeipnon. The after-supper service, the compline.

Apolytikion (pl. *apolytikia*). A hymn which sums up the subject of a holy day. It is chanted towards the end of the vespers and again at the orthros and the Divine Liturgy.

Arsanas (pl. *arsanades*). A landing place (harbor or pier) with warehouses and other buildings.

Ascesis. (Greek: *askesis.*) Methodical spiritual training, or discipline of the body and the soul, with a view to spiritual regeneration.

Ascetic. One who so disciplines himself, a spiritual striver. More narrowly, a monastic saint denoted in Greek by the term *hosios.* (See explanation of *hosios* below.)

Calophonic hirmos (pl. calophonic hirmi). A very artistic type of hymn requiring for its execution an exceptionally beautiful (*kalos*) voice (*phone*). Such hymns are chanted at the end of festal Liturgies, while the priest is giving *antidoron,* "holy bread," to the congregation.

Canon. A rule formulated and instituted by a Holy Synod (Council); also, a hymn consisting of many troparia and usually divided into eight odes, each of which is made up of the hirmos and three to six troparia, which are chanted like the hirmos. (For an explanation of the term *hirmos* see below.)

Cherubic Hymn. One of the slower hymns chanted during the
    Divine Liturgy, as the Bread and Wine of the Holy Eucharist
    are being prepared and brought from the offertory to the
    Holy Table. Its name is derived from the opening words: "We
    who mystically represent the Cherubim."
Communion Hymn. (Greek: *Koinonikon.*) One of the slower
    hymns chanted during the Divine Liturgy, as the priest is par-
    taking of the Holy Eucharist. A different Communion Hymn
    is chanted on Sunday, Monday, Tuesday, and each of the other
    days of the week.
Domestikos. A title formerly given both to the leading chanter of
    the right choir and to the leading chanter of the left choir.
Ecclesiarch. A monk who is in charge of the sacred relics, vessels,
    etc. in the sanctuary, and of the church (*ekklesia*) in general.
Eklogion. (From *eklego,* select.) A book containing selected lives
    of saints.
Epitaphios. A group of hymns and encomia commemorating the
    burial of Christ. They constitute part of the orthros of Good
    Saturday, and are chanted during the night of Good Friday.
First Cantor (Greek: *Protopsaltes*). The right cantor, or leader of
    the right choir. He leads the psalmodizing of a church, execut-
    ing more hymns than the left cantor, including the more im-
    portant and more difficult ones. The Byzantines called him the
    First Domestikos.
Great Horologion. (Greek: *Mega Horologion.*) One of the litur-
    gical books of the Orthodox Church, containing chiefly the
    offices for the nine canonical hours (*horai*), the *apolytikia* and
    kontakia for all the fixed holy days of the year as well as for
    the saints commemorated each day, and certain akoluthias or
    services such as the *Akathistos Hymn,* the canons of entreaty
    to the Theotokos, etc.
Hagiorite. (Greek: *Hagioreites.*) Of the Holy (*Hagion*) Moun-
    tain (*Oros*) or Mount Athos.
Heortodromion. The title of one of the books of Nicodemos the
    Hagiorite in which he interprets the canons of the feasts cele-
    brating major incidents in the life of Jesus and of the Theo-

tokos. The title is also used for books listing the holy days of the Church, or containing a collection of homilies on the excerpts from the Gospels or Epistles of St. Paul that are read on holy days, or homilies on the lives of the saints who are celebrated then.

Hesychasm. A term used to denote Eastern Orthodox mysticism, particularly the practice of mental prayer or prayer of the heart. It is derived from the word *hesychia,* which means quiet, stillness, because such prayer requires the greatest inner and outer quiet or stillness for its effective practice and the attainment of its ultimate goal, which is union with God. (See the explanation of the Jesus Prayer below.)

Hesychast. One who practices this form of prayer, an Orthodox mystic.

Hieromartyr. A martyr who was a priest or bishop.

Hieromonk. (Greek: *hieromonachos.*) Priest-monk.

Hirmos (pl. hirmi). The first stanza of an ode. It serves as the model for the structure and rhythm of the stanzas or troparia that follow.

Hosiomartyr. A martyr who was a monk.

Hosios (pl. *hosioi*). Holy, sacred; also, a monastic saint who did not suffer martyrdom but who distinguished himself for his holy life as an ascetic or spiritual striver.

Jesus Prayer. Mental prayer during which one invokes Jesus, saying: "Lord Jesus Christ, Son of God, have mercy upon me." This prayer is called "mental prayer" because it is carried on by the mind or rational faculty; "prayer of the heart," because the mind engages in it while concentrated in the heart or emotional center; and "pure prayer," because it presupposes a mind and heart free of fantasies, passions and thoughts.

Kalyva (pl. *kalyves*). An isolated cottage or hut.

Katabasiai (sing. *katabasia*). The first stanzas or the hirmi of the odes of a canon, making up a group of eight stanzas, except in the case of the *katabasiai* of the Nativity of Christ, of Theophany, and the Ascension and Pentecost, where there are sixteen hirmi, taken from two distinct canons.

Kelli (pl. *kellia*). The cell of a monk; also, a monastic establishment consisting of a building with a chapel in it and some surrounding land, and usually inhabited by three monks.

Komboskoini (pl. *komboskoinia*). Prayer rope, typically consisting of one hundred knots. At each knot (*kombos*) one says mentally a brief prayer, especially the Jesus Prayer.

Kontakion (pl. *kontakia*). A short hymn that summarizes the significance of the holy day or the praise of the saint that is celebrated. It is read at the orthros and chanted during the Liturgy.

Kratema (pl. *kratemata*). In Byzantine music, a melodious addition without words at the end of a long hymn. The place of words is taken by the syllables te-re-rem, or ne-na. *Kratema* also denotes a musical sign.

Logios (pl. *logioi*). Scholar.

Menaia (sing. *Menaion*). Twelve liturgical volumes, one for each month (*men*) of the year. In the Orthodox Church, each day of the month has a special vesper service and orthros, containing hymns for the saint or saints commemorated on that day; and hence each volume of this collection is divided into as many parts as the month for which it has been composed has days.

Myroblyte (Gr. *Myroblytes*). Certain saints are called *Myroblytai* (from *myron* — perfume, and *blyzo* — emit) because their relics give forth a fragrant odor or fluid.

New Rome. Constantinople, so called because it replaced Rome as the capital of the Roman Empire.

Orthros. Matins.

O. S. Old Style, according to the Old (Julian) Calendar. With the exception of Vatopedi, all the monasteries of the Holy Mountain and their dependencies follow the Old Calendar.

Pentekostarion. A liturgical book which contains the Easter Day service and the services for all subsequent movable holy days until the Sunday of All Saints — the Sunday after Pentecost.

Philokalia. A monumental anthology of writings by some thirty ascetic-mystical Fathers, ranging from the 4th to the 15th century, compiled by St. Macarios Notaras, Archbishop of Corinth, and edited by St. Nicodemos the Hagiorite. The full title of this work is *Philokalia of the Sacred Wakeful Individuals: Compiled from Our Holy and God-bearing Fathers, by Which the Mind is Purified, Illumined, and Perfected through Practical and Contemplative Ethical Philosophy.* The word *philokalia* means "love of the beautiful." This book has been so named because it is pervaded by the love of God viewed as the supremely beautiful Being and of the virtues viewed as qualities reflecting in us the beauty of God. The title *Philokalia* has also been given to a book — not referred to in the present work — compiled from the writings of Origen by Basil the Great and Gregory Nazianzen.

Prayer rope. See *komboskoini.*

Prosmonarios. The keeper of a church; one who waits for and receives those who come to worship.

Psalmodize. To execute vocally a Psalm or any other hymn of the Church, to chant.

Sacred lamp. (Greek: *kandeli.*) A small oil lamp placed — in a church usually suspended — before a holy icon.

Skete. Typically, a settlement of hermits in the neighborhood of a common church, known as the *kyriakon*, by which is the dwelling of the *dikaios* or prior of the settlement and a guesthouse. Also, a monastery-like monastic establishment that lacks the autonomy of a monastery. Both types of skete are dependencies of a monastery.

Theotokos. The Godbirthgiver, the All-Holy Virgin Mary, who gave birth to Christ in the form of man.

Theosis. Deification, union with God.

The Three Hierarchs. Basil the Great, Gregory Nazianzen, also known as Gregory the Theologian, and John Chrysostom.

Triodion. A liturgical book which contains the services for the Great Lent and the four weeks that precede it. The hymns in the book have reference to various events in the Old and the New Testaments, but especially to the Passion of Jesus.

Troparion. A hymn usually consisting of a single, rhythmic prose sentence. The term is especially used to denote the hymns of an ode other than the hirmi.

Typikon. A set of rules and regulations. In the case of a monastery, the rules and regulations for governing the brotherhood in all phases of its life.

SELECTED BIBLIOGRAPHY

Akolouthia ton Hosion kai Theophoron Pateron Hemon ton en to Hagio Orei tou Atho Dialampsanton ("Akoluthia of Our Holy and God-bearing Fathers Who Shone on the Holy Mountain of Athos"), ed. by Hieromonk Daniel and Monk Nectarios. Holy Mountain, 1941.

Ekklesia, bulletin of the Church of Greece, 1963, 1968, 1971-1973.

Eustratiadis, Sophronios, *Hagiologion tes Orthodoxou Ekklesias* ("Hagiology of the Orthodox Church"). Athens, 1960.

Fedotov, G. P., *The Russian Religious Mind,* Vol. 2, Cambridge, Mass., 1966.

Gabriel, Abbot of the Monastery of Dionysiou, *He en Hagio Orei Hiera Mone tou Hagiou Dionysiou* ("The Holy Monastery of Saint Dionysios on the Holy Mountain"). Athens, 1959.

Gedeon, Manuel, *Ho Athos ("Athos").* Constantinople, 1885.

Grunwald, Constantin de, *Saints of Russia.* New York, 1960.

Kourilas, Evlogios, Lavriotis, *Historia tou Asketismou: Athonitai* ("History of Asceticism: Athonites"), Vol. 1. Thessaloniki, 1929.

Megas Synaxaristes tes Orthodoxou Ekklesias ("Great Collection of Lives of Saints of the Orthodox Church"), ed. by Victor Matthaiou, 2nd ed., Athens, 1955-1962.

Migne, *Patrologia Graeca,* Vols. 150, 151, 154.

Nicodemos the Hagiorite, *Neon Martyrologion* ("New Martyrologium"). 3rd ed., Athens, 1961.

Papadopoulos, Chrysostomos, *Hoi Neomartyres* ("The Neomartyrs"). 3rd ed., Athens, 1970.

Papadopoulos, George I., *Symbolai eis ten Historian tes par Hemin Ekklesiastikes Mousikes* ("Contributions to the History of Our Ecclesiastical Music"). Athens, 1890.

——————*Historike Episkopesis tes Byzantines Ekklesiastikes Mousikes* ("Historical Survey of Byzantine Ecclesiastical Music"). Athens, 1904.

Philokalia, Vol. 4, Athens, 1961, Vol. 5, 1963.

Sathas, Constantine, *Neohellenike Philologia* ("Modern Greek Philology"). Athens, 1863.

Threskeutike kai Ethike Enkyklopaideia ("Religious and Ethical Encyclopedia"). Athens, 1962-1968.

Velimerovich, Nicholai, *The Life of Saint Sava.* Libertyville, Illinois, 1951.

Vretos, Andreas Papadopoulos, *Neohellenike Philologia* ("Modern Greek Philology"). Athens, 1854.

Zaviras, G. I., *Nea Hellas, e Hellenikon Theatron* ("Modern Greece, or the Greek Scene"). Athens, 1872.

INDEX

Africa, South, 59
afterlife, 31, 122
Agapios Landos, the Cretan, 17, 25-27, 33, 43, 70, 87
Agapios of Vatopedi, St., 150
Agathangelos of Esphigmenou, St., 150
agrypnia, 78; *see also* vigils
Akakios, hosiomartyr, 151
Akakios the Younger, of Kafsokalyvitis, St., 63, 66-68, 149, 150, 152
Akindynos, Gregory, 21, 22
akoluthia, 22, 28, 33, 54, 59, 87, 89, 90, 154, 155
Albania, 57, 69, 152, 153
America, 48, 59, 115, 128
analogion, 80
Anastasia Pharmakolytria, St., 110
antidoron, 124, 154
anti-monasticism, 112-113, 117-120, 125, 128, 130, 131, 132
antiphony, 80
Antony Pechersky, St., 43-44, 51, 152
Antony the Great, St., 66
apodeipnon, 78, 83, 89, 111, 154
apologetics, 24

apolytikion, 21, 33, 48, 52, 54-55, 68, 90, 154, 155
Aristotle, 23, 29, 108
arsanas, 121, 154
Arsenios the Younger, St., 90, 153
Arseny, Archbishop of Serbia, 47
ascesis, 39, 154
"ascetic," 62-63, 154
Athanasios the Athonite, St., 63-64, 77, 78, 152
Athanasios the Younger, St., 147
Athonias Academy, 57, 105
attention, inner, 18, 19, 20, 21, 40, 71, 73, 82
Augustine Kantiotis, 26, 111, 144
Augustine, St., 108-109
Australia, 59, 94

Bairaktaris, Styl. S., 134
Balkans, 23, 31
Barlaam, monk of Calabria, 21, 22
Barsanuphios, St., 52
Bartholomew of Koutloumousiou, 17, 34-35

Basil Ivanovich, Czar, 24
Basil the Great, St., 22, 30, 38, 52, 60, 77, 118, 158
beards, 108-109
Bekkos, John, Patriarch, 61, 113-114, 146, 148-149, 151
belief, true, 62
bells, 111
Berdyaev, 39, 138
Bereketis, see Glykys
body, 73, 83, 154
Bogdania, 31
Bogomils, 47
Bucharest, 28, 29, 30
Bulgaria, 90, 106, 149
Bulgarian Monastery, see Zographou
Bulgarians, 15, 78, 146
Byzantine hymnography, 78-90
Byzantine iconography, 27-28, 102, 110-111
Byzantine music, 79-90, 121
Byzantium, 85, 90, 132

Callistos Xanthopoulos, St., 17, 22, 82, 83, 148, 151
calophonic hirmi, 85, 88, 154
Calvinism, 29
canonarchema, 80-81
Canon Law, 29, 30, 33
canons, holy, 29, 30, 38, 113, 127, 154
canons, musical, 86, 87, 89, 90, 154, 156
Cantacuzenos, John, Emperor, 65-66
Capodistrias, John, 40-41
cares, freedom from, 18, 100
catechisms, 58
Cavarnos, C., 133, 135, 136, 137, 138, 139, 140, 141, 142, 143
chanters, 80, 81, 85, 86, 88-90, 155

chanting, 73, 77-84, 102, 106, 121, 158
Cherubic Hymn, 85, 87, 88, 155
choirs, 80-81, 90
choros, 80
Choukas, Michael, 128
Christ, 18, 19, 79, 86, 100, 106, 112, 116, 117, 118, 124-125, 155, 156, 158
Christodoulidis, Sapphiros, 57, 58
Christophoros Artinos, 88, 89
Christophoros of Dionysiou, St., 150
Christou, Panayotis, 133
Chrysanthos Aitolos, 32
Chrysanthos, Patriarch of Jerusalem, 67
Chrysotomos Papadopoulos, 160
Church Fathers, see Fathers
Church, Orthodox, 16, 19, 20, 24, 116-117, 124
Climacos, John, see John Climacos
coenobitic monasticism, 28, 63, 77, 97, 111, 129
coenobium, 63, 126
commandments, Divine, 55, 66, 118
Communion, Holy, 29, 36, 41, 120, 122, 126-127, 138, 155
Communion Hymns, 82, 85, 87, 88, 155
compline, see apodeipnon
concentration, 52, 73, 83, 118
confession, 17, 30, 33, 37, 38, 54, 73, 120
consciousness, 83-84
Constantinople, 20, 21, 29, 30, 31, 32, 35, 40, 50, 54, 56, 57, 63, 66, 69, 85, 87, 88, 89, 90, 113, 146-153
Constantios the Russian, St., 148

contemplation (*theoria*), 20, 66, 71
contentment, 100, 102
continence, 73
contrition, 82, 86, 121
Cosmas Aitolos, St., 32, 43, 56-59, 109, 111-112, 153
Cosmas of Iviron, 87
Cosmas of the Skete of St. Anne, St., 148
Cosmas the Bulgarian, St., 146
Council of Lyon, Second, 19
counseling, 17, 43, 46, 66, 67, 73
Cross, Holy, 41, 97, 110
Cucuzelis, *see* Koukouzelis
Cyprian of Koutloumousiou, 43, 55, 152
Cyril, Archbishop of Tinos, 88
Cyril of Alexandria, St., 31

Dalmatia, 48
Damaskinos of Hilandari, St., 149
Damaskinos of Lavra, St., 148
Damian of Esphigmenou, St., 149
Damian of Lavra, St., 148
Damian of Philotheou, St., 43, 55, 149
Damian of Vatopedi, 87-88
Daniel of Tyrnavos, 88
Daphne, port of, 94, 95, 96, 101, 110
Dapontes, Kaisarios, *see* Kaisarios
David of the Skete of St. Anne, St., 152
Dawkins, R. M., 81
Dendrinos, Procopios, *see* Procopios Dendrinos
Dentakis, B. L., 133-134
Desert Fathers, 37, 47, 136
diamoneterion, 101
Didron, Adolphe, 28, 134-135

dikaios, 122, 123, 158
Dionysios of Fourna, 17, 27-28, 43
Dionysios of Iviron, St., 147
Dionysios of Olympos, St., 149
Dionysios the Hagiorite, St., 151-152
Dionysios the Orator, St., 40, 90, 152
Dionysiou, Monastery of, 32, 33, 36-38, 49, 60, 105, 115-120, 130, 146, 147, 151-152, 160
Docheiariou, Monastery of, 3, 54, 96, 147, 153
dogmatics, 20, 24
Domestikos, 155
Dometios of Dionysiou, St.; 152
Dometios of Philotheou, St., 149, 153
Dorotheos, Abba, 52
Doukakis, Constantine, 17, 35-36

Ecclesiarch, 110, 155
"Ecumenism," vii, 41, 113, 116, 124, 131
effulgence, 20, 21, 33
Egypt, 66
Eklogion, 26, 155
emotions, 83, 100, 122, 123
encomia, 22
Ephraim, hieromonk, 72, 124-125, 129
Ephraim the Syrian, St., 40
Epitaphios, 89, 155
Esphigmenou, Monastery of, 20, 44, 147, 150, 152
epistemonarches, 78
ethics, 24, 29, 33, 37, 119
Eucharist, *see* Communion
Eustratiadis, Sophronios, 61, 142, 160
Euthymios of Docheiariou, St., 147

Euthymios of Iviron's Skete of Prodromou, St., 150, 151
Euthymios of Vatopedi, St., 148
Euthymios the Iberian, St., 151
Euthymios the Younger St., 147
Evdokimos, abbot of Xenophontos, 131
Evdokimos of Vatopedi, St., 147
Evergetinos, 37, 130, 136
Evlogios Kourilas, 69, 140, 160
experience, 20-21

faith, 18, 49, 50, 66, 116, 122, 123, 127, 132, 138
fasting, 46, 73, 120
Fathers, Greek, 18, 28, 36, 38, 39, 40, 45, 46, 51-52, 60, 79, 117, 119, 127
Fedotov, G. P., 52, 54, 160
First Cantor, 85, 86, 88-89, 155
Florovsky, Georges, 133
foreknowledge, 67
freedom, 53, 100
French, R. M., 134

Gabriel, abbot of Dionysiou, 17, 27, 36-38, 49, 50, 59, 105, 107, 115-119, 120, 160
Gabriel of Iviron, St., 151
Gazis, Theodore, 29
Gedeon, Manuel, 35, 85, 86, 90, 137, 139, 160
Gedeon of Karakallou, St., 148
Gennadios of Dionysiou, St., 150
Gennadios of Vatopedi, St., 148
George the Iberian, St., 151
George the Orator, 37
Gerasimos Halkiopoulos, 87
Gerasimos Mikragiannanitis, 33, 90
Gerasimos of Cephalonia, St., 70, 71-72
Gerasimos of the Skete of Panteleimonos, St., 152

Germanos of Lavra, 22
Gerontikon, 130
Gerontios, St., 153
Glykis, Peter, 88-89, 90
God, 18, 20, 23, 45, 48, 54, 57, 60, 62, 64, 66, 71, 73, 77, 79, 82, 86, 87, 99, 107, 112, 116, 117, 118, 120, 121, 122, 127, 131, 142, 156, 158
grace, Divine, 18, 21, 58, 60, 67, 71, 83
Great Horologion, 34, 155
Greeks, 15, 34, 36, 57-58, 132
Gregoras, Nikephoros, 22
Gregory Byzantios, St., 150
Gregory Nazianzen, St., 22, 38, 77, 110, 158
Gregory, founder of Grigoriou, St., 149
Gregory of Nyssa, St., 125
Gregory Palamas, Archbishop of Thessaloniki, St., 17, 18, 19, 20-21, 22, 39, 40, 87, 133, 148
Gregory the Domestikos, St., 86, 147
Gregory the Sinaite, St., 22, 52, 65-66
Gregory V, Patriarch of Constantinople, 42
Grigoriou, Monastery of, 110-114, 126, 130, 148
Grunwald, de, Constantin, 53, 139, 160
guarding of the heart, 18
guarding of the mind, 52

Halatzoglous, Panayotis, 88, 89, 90
Halkiopoulos, Gerasimos, *see* Gerasimos Halkiopoulos
handicrafts, 67, 71, 123-125
happiness, 100, 122
health, 102, 126
heart, 18, 77, 83, 105, 156

hell, 62
Heortodromion, 79, 155-156
heroism, 112-113
hesychasm, 156; see also mysticism
hesychast, 156
hieromartyr, 156
hieromonk, 156
Hierotheos of Iviron, St., 40
Hierotheos the Younger, St., 146
Hilandari, Monastery of, 46, 48, 128, 149
hirmos, 88, 154, 156, 159
Hodges, H. A., 33
holiness, 16, 117, 122, 125
Holy Community, 101, 106, 129
Homer, 108
homophony, 79-80
hope, 123
hosiomartyr, 114, 156
hosios, 62, 154, 156
humility, 49, 64, 65, 71, 82, 118
hymnographers, vii, 77, 85
hymnography, 20, 27, 33, 77-90
hymns, 19, 21, 22, 24-25, 27, 31, 33, 48, 49, 52, 77, 81, 82, 83, 85, 86, 87, 88, 89, 111, 142, 154, 155, 157, 158

Iakovos of Iviron, St., 43, 53-55, 147
iconography, 28-29, 79, 102, 105, 110-111, 123, 138
iconostasis, 99, 102, 105, 111, 121, 122, 124
idiorrhythmic monasticism, 97, 129
Ignatios of Iviron's Skete of Prodromou, St., 147
Ignatios Xanthopoulos, 17, 22, 82, 83
ignorance, 57, 58
Ilarion of the Skete of St. Anne, St., 146

illumination, 18, 20, 24, 45, 46, 54, 63, 65, 67, 71, 83
Illyricum, 48
imagination, 83, 105
injustice, 55
Innocent of Okhlyabinin, St., 51
intellect, 20, 21
Isaac the Syrian, St., 130
Isidore, Patriarch, 22
Islam, 24, 57, 62
Italy, 18, 23
Iviron, Monastery of, 15, 40, 43, 54, 59, 60, 87, 89, 135, 146, 151

James, William, 100
Joasaph of Dionysiou, St., 43, 50, 147
John Chrysostom, St., 22, 38, 87, 158
John Climacos, St., 52, 73, 80, 130
John Damascene, St., 85
John of Trebizond, 88
John the Iberian, St., 151
Johnstone, John, Jr., viii
Jonas of Kafsokalyvia, 68
Joseph of Dionysiou, St., 146
Joseph the Hesychast, 63, 69-72, 124, 125, 129
Judaism, 24
justice, 66

Kafsokalyvia, Skete of, 28, 30, 64, 68, 69, 150
Kaisarios Dapontes, 17, 30-32, 33, 88, 89
kalyva, 123, 124, 156
kanonarches, 80-81
Kantiotis, Augustine, *see* Augustine Kantiotis
Karakallou, Monastery of, 148
Karatzas, Theocletos, *see* Theocletos Karatzas

katabasiai, 87, 156
katholikon, 80, 97
Karyes, 15, 46, 63, 72, 96, 101, 104, 105, 108, 109, 148
kelli, 79, 99, 101, 106, 124, 129, 157
Kiev, 43, 44, 152
kneelings, 46, 73
Kollyvades, 29, 127
komboskoinia, 124-125, 157, 158
kontakion, 56, 59, 64, 66, 86, 90, 155, 157
Kontoglou, Fotis, 42, 132, 138
Koukouzelis, John, St., 85-86, 147
Kourilas, Evlogios, *see* Evlogios
Koutloumousiou, Monastery of, 35, 43, 56, 102, 108-109, 128, 152
kratema, 82, 88, 157
Kritopoulos, Metrophanis, 41
Krivosheine, Vasilii, *see* Vasilii
kyriakon, 15, 121, 158

Landos, Agapios, *see* Agapios Landos
Laourdas, Basil, 132
Laskaris, Theodore, Emperor, 47
Lausaikon, 130
Lavra, Monastery of, 15, 20, 22, 25, 28, 60, 63, 64, 69, 72, 78, 85, 86, 87, 89, 94, 106, 115, 147, 148, 150, 151, 152
Legrand, Emile, 31
Leontiev, Constantine, 42, 138
Leontios the Hagiorite, St., 151
Liturgy, 31, 78, 81, 97, 113, 121, 122, 123, 124, 154, 155, 157
Loch, Sidney, 94-95
logios, 17, 157
Louvaris, Nicholas, 132
love (*agape*), 17, 25, 35, 46, 53, 59, 64, 65, 66, 67, 71, 73, 102, 117-118, 120, 122
Luke of the Skete of St. Anne,

St., 150
Macarios Makris, St., 149
Macarios of Corinth, St., 36, 41, 50, 158
Macarios of Dionysiou, St., 43, 50, 146
Macarios of the Skete of St. Anne, St., 147
Manuel I, Patriarch of Constantinople, St., 47
martyrs, 36, 43, 51, 54-62, 68-69, 114, 146, 148, 149, 151, 160
materialism, 132
matins, *see orthros*
Maximos Kafsokalyvitis, St., 63, 64-66, 69, 149, 151
Maximos the Greek, or Maximos of Vatopedi, 17, 23-25, 43, 53, 149
meditation, 46, 52, 73
meekness, 100, 116
megalynaria, 90
Menaia, 34-35, 157
Meteora, 54
Metrophanis Kritopoulos, 41
Metrophanis, St., 152
Meyendorff, John, 133
Michael Maleinos, St., Monastery of, 63
mind, 18, 20, 65, 71, 73, 82, 105, 156, 157
miracles, 21, 25, 55, 58, 63, 66, 68, 70, 132
mirrors, 108, 109
missionaries, vii, 15-16, 17, 23-24, 25, 28, 43-59, 60, 73, 111-112
Moldavia, 31, 135
Molinos, de, Miguel, 40
monasticism, vii, 17, 19, 24, 37, 38, 39, 43-44, 51-53, 77-79, 107, 108, 112-113, 117-120, 122, 125, 128-132, 134

morality, *see* ethics
Moskos, John, 36
Moscow, 53
music, vii, 77-90, 98, 111, 121, 141, 161
musical instruments, 78-79
musicians, vii, 85
myroblyte, 157
mysticism, 17, 18, 19, 20, 21, 22, 40, 51-52, 65, 69-72, 83, 156

Nectarios Kephalas, St., 41, 90
Nectarios of the Kelli of Iagri, St., 148
Nectarios of the Skete of St. Anne, St., 153
Nectarios Vlachos, 89
Nemanya, Stephen, 45
Neophytos Kafsokalyvitis, 17, 28-29, 33, 88, 89
Neophytos of Docheiariou, St., 147
Neophytos of Vatopedi, St., 149
Nestor, 43
New Skete, 41, 69, 70, 72, 89, 123-125
Nicaea, 19, 47
Nicholas, St., 87
Nicodemos the Albanian, St., 69, 152
Nicodemos the Hagiorite, St., 17, 18, 23, 32-33, 36, 39, 40, 49, 50, 55, 56, 66, 79, 82, 83, 88, 89, 90, 101-103, 109, 136, 143, 153, 157, 160
Nicodemos the Younger, St., 22
Nikephoros Theotokis, 123-124
Nikephoros the Solitary, St., 17-19, 151
Niketas of the Skete of St. Anne, St., 150
Nikon, hermit of Karoulia, 95, 143

Nilos the Myroblyte, St., 147, 151
Nil Sorsky, St., 43, 51-53, 151
Niphon, disciple of Maximos Kafsokalyvitis, St., 66, 151
Niphon, Patriarch of Constantinople, St., 43, 48-50, 54, 153

obedience, 44
Oikonomos, Constantine, 29
Onouphrios of Hilandari, St., 149
orthros, 78, 81, 83, 96, 97, 111, 121, 154, 155, 157

Pachomios of Russia, St., 69, 151
Palaiologos, Andronikos II, 19, 20, 86
Palaiologos, John, Emperor, 65
Palaiologos, Michael, Emperor, 19, 61, 146, 148-149, 151
Palamas, *see* Gregory Palamas
Panagiotopoulos, D. G., 141
Panselinos, Manuel, 63
Panteleimonos, Monastery of, 17, 29, 36, 39, 40, 45, 79, 96, 99, 128, 129-130, 151
Panteleimonos, Skete of, 152
Pantocratoros, Monastery of, 22, 49, 150, 152
Papademetriou, George C., 133
Papadopoulos, Chrysostomos, *see* Chrysostomos
Papadopoulos, George I., 86, 140, 141, 142, 161
Papamichael, Gregory, 25
Parios, Athanasios, 41-42
passionlessness, 100
passions, 67, 100, 109, 122, 126-127, 131, 156
Paul of Lavra, St., 151
Paul of Xeropotamou, St., 153
peace of soul, 46
Pechersk Monastery, 43, 44

Pentekostarion, 34-35, 157
perfection, 20, 23, 46, 57, 62, 73, 117, 119-120
Pericles, 108
Peter the Athonite, St., 151
Philokalia, 18, 19, 20, 23, 33, 65, 130, 157-158, 161
philosophy, 29, 34, 132
    ancient Greek, 29
    ascetic, spiritual, 18, 19-20
Philotheos, founder of Philotheou, St., 149
Philotheos of Dionysiou, St., 147
Philotheos of Karyes, St., 148
Philotheos the Patriarch, 17, 19, 21-22, 87, 133-134, 147
Phocas, Nikephoros, 63
Plato, 23, 108, 109
polyphony, 79
poverty, 53, 100
practices,
    mental, 46, 51, 52, 73, 83, 131
    physical, 46, 73, 83
prayer, 18-19, 23, 32, 45, 46, 51, 64, 65, 67, 73, 77, 82, 83, 85, 87, 102, 106, 120, 132, 142
    Jesus Prayer, 18, 67, 71, 106, 156
    mental or spiritual, 18, 19, 21, 22, 40, 45, 51, 52, 65, 66, 67, 69, 71-72, 83, 131, 156
    of the heart, 156
preaching, 17, 23-24, 43, 49, 50, 54, 55, 57-58, 62
Procopios Dendrinos, 40
Procopios, St., 152
Prodromou, Iviron's Skete of, 54, 89, 147, 150
Prodromou, Rumanian Skete of, 70, 89
prophecy, gift of, 54, 65-66
Prophet Elijah, Skete of, 107, 128
prosmonarios, 158

protopsaltes, 155
Pruden, Leo M., viii
Psachos, K. A., 142
psalmodizing, see chanting
purification, 83, 119, 120, 122, 131
purity, 33, 118, 125

quietness (hesychia), 20, 65, 83, 85, 97-98, 109, 127, 131

rational faculty, 83, 156
reading, 73
Reformation, Western, 24
renunciation, 20, 31, 44, 45, 52, 117
repentance, 120, 131
Romanides, John, 133
Romanos of Karpenisi, St., 69, 149
Rumania, 26
Rumanians, 15, 78, 99-100
Russia, 24, 43-44, 51-54, 59, 69, 106-107, 129-130
Russian Monastery, see Panteleimonos
Russians, 15, 78, 79, 104-107

saint, concept of, 60
saints, vii, viii, 15-16, 20-21, 22, 26, 32, 33, 36, 38, 40, 43, 51, 60-72, 73, 86, 89, 114, 122, 124, 125, 146-153, 155, 156
salutations, 89
salvation, 21, 33, 44, 51, 54, 65, 73, 114, 119, 120
Sardelis, Kostas, 58
Sathas, Constantine, 134, 138, 161
Sava of Serbia, St., 43, 45-48, 149
Savvas of Vatopedi, 22
Schoinas, Soterios, 69
scholars, vii, 15-42, 60, 73

schools, 57

Scripture, 21, 38, 41, 119, 123-124, 127

semantron, 97, 111

senses, 83

Serbia, 43, 45, 46

Serbian Monastery, *see* Hilandari

Serbs, 15, 78, 79

serenity, 100, 111, 116

Silouan, Staretz, 41

Simon the Athonite, St., 82

Simon the Myroblyte, St., 148

Simonopetra, Monastery of, 82, 110, 148, 150

sin, 41, 100, 112, 115

sketes, 15, 51, 53, 78, 79, 80, 104, 158

Small Skete of St. Anne, 25, 40, 70, 152

Smyrna, 32

Sophronios of the Skete of St. Anne, St., 153

Sofrony, Archimandrite, 40, 41

solitude, 63, 65, 130

soul, 31, 40, 73, 77, 78, 83, 120, 122, 132, 154

Spetsieris, Joachim, 40, 41

spiritual combat, 52

St. Andrew, Skete of, 104-107, 128

St. Anne Skete of, 40,121, 122, 146, 147, 148, 150, 152, 153

St. Basil, Skete of, 129

St. Paul, Monastery of, 40, 41, 63-64, 69, 72, 97, 123, 128-129, 153

Stathis, Gregory, 141

Stavronikita, Monastery of, 129

Stokes, Margaret, 28, 134-135

Studenitza, Monastery of, 45-47

Studium, Monastery of, 77-78

Symeon Metaphrastis, 26

Symeon of Philotheou, St., 43, 55-56, 150

Symeon Nemanya, St., 45-47, 149

Symeon of Thessaloniki, 23

Symeon the New Theologian, St., 38, 39, 40, 52, 130

Synesios the Hagiorite, 87

Synod of Florence, 48

Synods, 21, 29, 30, 116, 127, 154

Thekaras, Theodoulos, 86-87, 141-142

Theocletos Karatzas, 17, 29-30

Theocletos of Dionysiou, 17, 33, 36, 38-39, 115, 119-120, 131

Theocletos of Iviron, 40

Theodore the Studite, St., 77

Theodoret of Cyrus, 26

Theodoretos of St. Anne, 41, 138

Theodosios of Philotheou, St., 149

Theodosios of St. Paul's, 40, 126-127

Theodosius of Russia, St., 43, 44

Theoleptos, Metropolitan of Philadelphia, 17, 18, 19-20, 82, 83-84, 86

theology, 20, 51, 79, 113, 119, 132

Theonas, St., 150

Theophanes of Docheiariou, St., 153

Theophanes of Vatopedi, 66

Theophan the Recluse, Bishop, 33

Theophilos the Myroblyte, St., 152

theosis, 73, 158

Theotokarion, 89

Theotokis, Nikephoros, *see* Nikephoros Theotokis

Theotokis of Vatopedi, 89

Theotokos, 40, 86, 87, 89, 99-100, 121, 125, 131, 142, 155, 156, 158

Thessaloniki, 15, 18, 21, 50, 54, 56, 57, 59, 64, 93-94, 102, 104, 132, 150, 151, 152
thoughts, 83, 122, 156
time, Byzantine, 96-97, 143
Timothy of Esphigmenou, St., 147
Thucydides, 29
tourism, 94, 101, 108, 109, 128, 129, 130-131
Tradition, 39, 116-117
Transylvania, 101
Triodion, 34, 158
troparion, 81, 87, 90, 154, 156, 158-159
truth, 62, 66
Typikon, 63, 68, 159

Vasilii Krivosheine, 17, 36, 39-40, 133
Vatopedi, Monastery of, 15, 20, 23, 28, 45, 46, 49, 60, 61, 66, 88, 89, 104, 106, 147, 148, 149, 150, 157
Velichkovsky, Paissy, 26
Velimerovich, Nicholai, 48, 161
Venice, 25, 33, 87
Venizelos, Eleftherios, 131
vespers, 78, 81, 87, 111, 121, 154
Victor Matthaiou, 160
vigils, 73, 78, 86, 89, 120, 121

virtue, 33, 44, 49, 50, 60, 66, 71, 122, 127, 157
visions, spiritual, 44, 67
Vissarion, abbot of Grigoriou, 111-114, 116
Voulgaris, Eugene, 41
Voutieridis, Elias P., 136
Vretos, Andreas Papadopoulos, 161
Vryennios, Joseph, 117

wakefulness, inner, 18-19
Wallachia, 29, 30, 31, 49, 89
Whitman, Walt, 100
wisdom, spiritual, 20, 25, 66
women, 31-32, 118, 130
"work," *see* practices
"world," the, 31, 112-113, 115, 118-120, 130-132
worship, 73, 78, 80, 93, 121

Xanthopoulos, *see* Callistos and Ignatios Xanthopoulos
Xenophontos, Monastery of, 96, 131, 135
Xeropotamou, Monastery of, 31, 89, 96-98, 99, 101, 153

Zaviras, G. I., 25, 30, 135, 141-152, 161
"Zoe" Brotherhood, 119-120
Zographou, Monastery of, 60, 61, 96, 114, 146